Statistics and Probability Grades 5-6
Table of Contents

Children naturally like to explore. They observe, question, manipulate, organize, and communicate information in an effort to understand the relationship between themselves and their world. The study of statistics and probability is appropriate for students of this age, because this curiosity naturally encourages the growth of these mathematical skills and processes. Introduction of graphs and charts at this age also contributes to a solid grasp of statistics since children can see relationships between items and events. Probability exploration is a fun, concrete learning experience for students. Moreover, the study of statistics and probability enhances the development of problem-solving skills as students interpret data and use the information to predict activities and outcomes based on these facts.

The National Council of Teachers of Mathematics recommends that a statistics and probability curriculum teach not only reading and interpreting graphs, but that it also be used to help students understand how this knowledge can be used in other areas to describe and interpret the world around them. Statistics and probability skills can be carried into other curriculum areas, too, such as reading population growth charts in social studies or comparing circle graphs of endangered species in science.

ORGANIZATION
Statistics and Probability Grades 5-6 is divided into three units.

Tables and Data
In this section, students learn how to read and interpret a variety of tables. While most tables are charts and tally tables, students also explore schedules, logic tables, and number pattern tables. They are introduced to the concept of samples in surveys and the importance of choosing an appropriate group. Students also work with the statistical skills of finding the mean, median, mode, and range in a set of numbers.

Graphs
Students have the opportunity to explore a variety of graphs. They use and make pictographs, bar graphs, line graphs, circle graphs, and grid graphs. Within these graphs, they discover different scales and ways to display data for others to use and interpret. Questions for graph interpretation extend the thought process so that students try to discover the reason that data changes or find ways the data can be used.

Probability
Students are just beginning to understand the concepts of predicting and chances. This section offers a full range of probability experiences. Students learn about favorable outcomes, frequency, and proportion. They test predictions of spinner games, number cubes, and choosing an object from a group. They practice calculating mathematical outcomes and compare them to experimental outcomes to predict probability. Students are also introduced to the concepts of combinations, permutations, factorials, and tree diagrams.

SPECIAL FEATURES
Worksheet Pages
Each worksheet serves as practice for one basic skill. At the top of each page is an introduction to or a reminder of the important ideas of the skill on the page. Worksheets that introduce the skill guide students through the process.

Other pages are simply practice pages. Each page in *Statistics and Probability Grades 5-6* ends with an Extension exercise. These exercises offer students the opportunity to work on the skill at a higher level or suggest that students look for examples of how the skill is used in real life. Some Extension activities could require the use of a calculator and are marked with a calculator icon to signal its use.

Blackline Masters
Copies of blank graphs are included on pages 8 through 12 of *Statistics and Probability Grades 5-6*. These graphs include pictographs, horizontal and vertical bar graphs, line graphs, circle graphs, and grid graphs. The blacklines can be used in a variety of ways.

- Make a transparency for the overhead to guide students through an exercise.
- Make copies for assignments for which students need another graph. (Some Extension activities require students to make new graphs.)
- Make a copy for students who could benefit from the use of larger visuals or who need a larger work area due to motor-skill development.

Use
This book is designed to enhance your existing statistics and probability curriculum. Copies of the worksheets can be given to individuals, pairs of students, or small groups for completion. The worksheets can also be given as homework for reviewing and reinforcing these mathematics skills.

To begin, determine the implementation that fits your students' needs and your classroom structure. The following plan suggests a format for use:

1. Administer the Assessment Tests to establish baseline information on each student. These tests may also be used as post-tests to see if students have mastered the skills.
2. Explain the purpose of the worksheets to your class.
3. Review the mechanics of how you want students to do the exercises.
4. Introduce students to the process and purpose of the activities. Work with students when they have difficulty. Give them only a few pages at a time to avoid pressure.
5. Discuss how students can use the skill as they work and play.

Additional Notes
1. A NCTM Standards Correlation for Statistics and Probability can be found on page 5. This page identifies the target skill or skills that correspond to the standards.
2. A Curriculum Correlation chart can be found on page 6. It will help with cross-curricular lesson planning.
3. A Letter to Parents is included on page 7. Send it home with the students and encourage them to share it with their parents.
4. Have fun with the pages. Math should be an enjoyable adventure that helps students grow, not only in math but also in their confidence and their ability to face new and challenging experiences.

NCTM Standards Correlation for Statistics and Probability

STATISTICS
Collect Data
	(Pages)
Conduct surveys	33, 34

Organize and Interpret Data
Make predictions	17, 31, 32, 33, 50, 53, 57, 59, 72, 76
Make inferences	18, 19, 20, 29, 30, 31, 32, 34, 37, 38, 40, 43, 45, 46, 54, 56, 57, 60, 69, 74, 87
Make evaluations	17, 30, 31, 33, 44, 45, 75
Make and read tally chart	27, 28, 29, 32, 33, 34, 72, 74, 77
Make and read tables	16, 17, 18, 19, 20, 21, 22, 23, 24, 25, 26, 35, 42, 45, 46, 48, 49, 51, 55, 56, 61, 75, 76, 86
Find mean	35, 36, 49, 56
Find median	38
Find mode	37
Find range	39, 46, 53

Graphing
Read and make pictographs	40, 41, 42, 43, 69
Read and make bar graphs	44, 45, 46, 47, 48, 49, 50, 51, 52, 69
Read and make line graphs	53, 54, 55, 56, 57, 58, 69
Read and make circle graphs	59, 60, 61, 62, 63, 69
Read and make grid graphs	64, 65, 66, 67, 68, 69
Compare graphs	43, 52, 57, 58, 63, 69

PROBABILITY
Concept Development
Make predictions	70, 71, 72, 73, 75, 76, 77, 79, 81, 82, 86
Understand certainty	82
Understand real-world application	73, 74, 79, 80, 83, 86, 92

Experiments
Mathematical probability	72, 73, 75, 76, 77, 78, 79, 80, 81, 83, 84, 84, 86, 89, 91
Compare mathematical and experimental data	72, 77, 78, 80, 92
Combinations and permutations	83, 84, 85, 86, 87, 88, 89, 90
Tree diagrams	85
Word problems	83, 90, 92

Curriculum Correlation

	TABLES AND DATA	GRAPHING	PROBABILITY
Language Arts	35	43, 48, 66	74, 81
Science	13, 16, 26, 38	41, 46, 50, 52, 53, 58, 60, 61	76, 79, 86
Social Studies	14, 15, 18, 21, 29, 34, 39	40, 42, 44, 45, 49, 55, 56, 57, 59, 62, 63, 64, 65, 66, 67	70, 71, 72, 73, 75, 76, 77, 78, 80, 82, 83, 84, 88, 89, 91, 92
Physical Education	17, 19, 23, 36, 37	48, 49	85
Health/Nutrition	20, 22, 24, 25, 27, 28, 30, 31, 32	51	87
Art/Music	33	54, 63	90

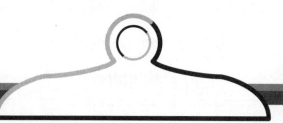

Dear Parent,

During the year, your child will be learning and practicing mathematics skills which involve statistics and probability. Some of the skills include reading and making tables, pictographs, bar graphs, line graphs, circle graphs, and grid graphs. Students will also explore probability in a concrete, hands-on method. After exploring the concepts associated with these basic skills, your child may bring home worksheets designed to further practice these skills. To best help your child, please consider the following suggestions:

- Provide a quiet place to work.
- Read directions together.
- Encourage your child to do his or her best.
- Review the lesson when it is complete, noting improvements as well as problems.

Help your child maintain a positive attitude about these mathematics skills. Point out examples in everyday experiences where statistics and probability are used. You could challenge your child to predict the chances of rolling a number in a board game. While reading a newspaper or magazine, point out graphs you find. Also, have your child list possible food combinations that could be served for dinner.

Thank you for your help. Your child and I appreciate your assistance and reinforcement in this learning process.

Cordially,

Pictograph

Title: _____

Pictures

Category:						
___						
___						

Scale: _____

Name _____   Date _____

Vertical Bar Graph

Title: _____

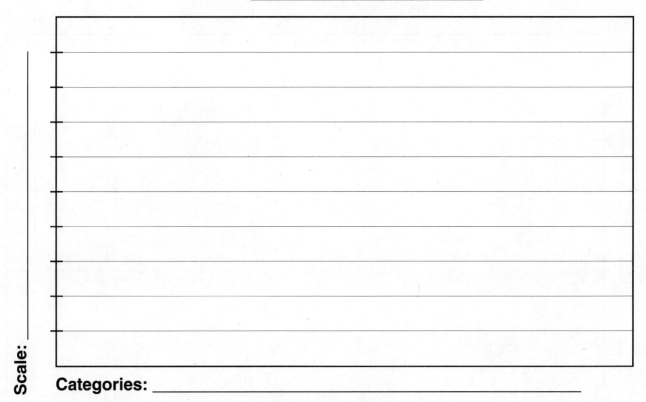

Scale:

Categories: _____

Horizontal Bar Graph

Title: _____

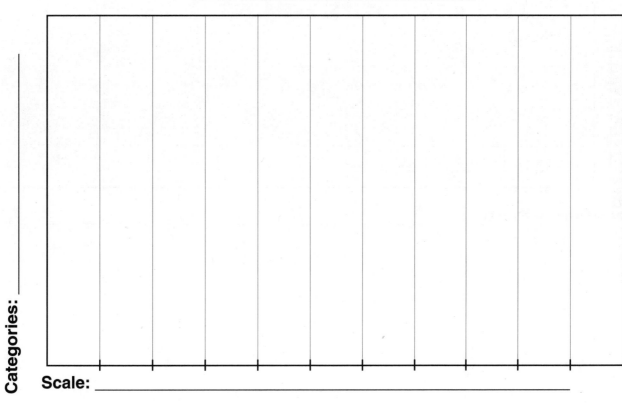

Categories:

Scale: _____

9   Statistics and Probability 5-6, SV 7479-0

Name _____   Date _____

Line Graph

Title: _____

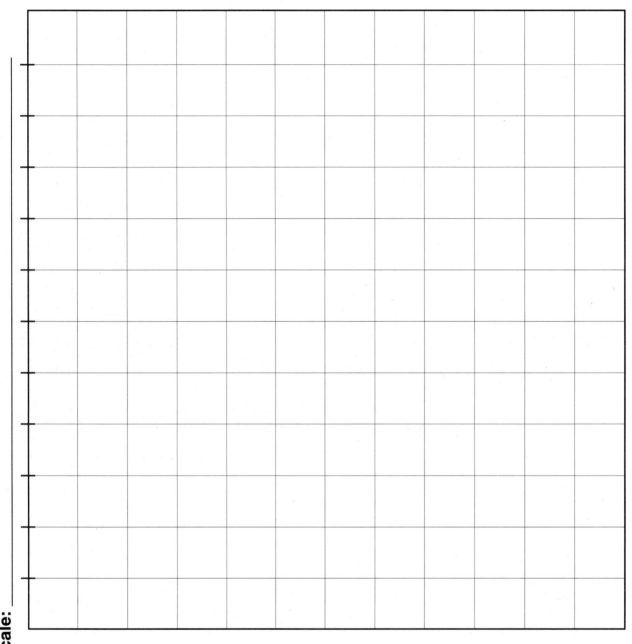

Scale: ___

Time of Change: _____

Name _____   Date _____

Circle Graph

Title: _____

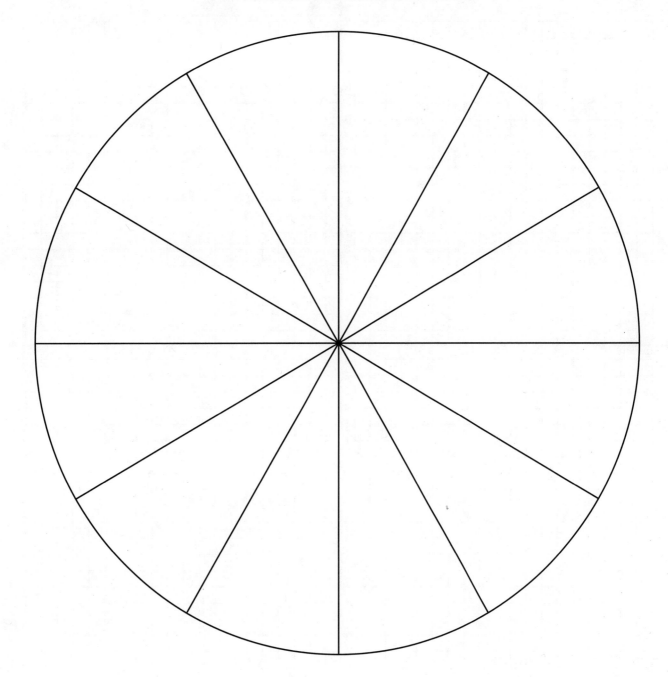

Statistics and Probability 5-6, SV 7479-0

Name _____   Date _____

Grid Graph

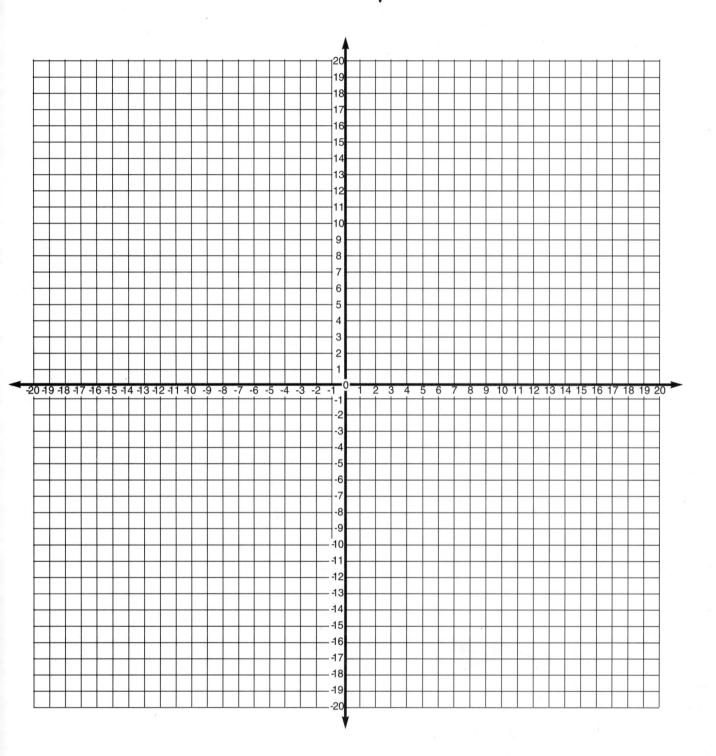

    Statistics and Probability 5-6, SV 7479-0

Name _____ Date _____

Table Talk

Macy recorded the temperatures in Chicago for several weeks. They were as follows: 21°, 25°, 16°, 18°, 18°, 26°, 21°, 17°, 19°, 21°, 22°, 24°, 26°, 21°, 22°, 17°, 16°, 17°, 21°, and 25°F. Make a graph to show the data.

1. Make a tally and frequency table to show the data.

2. How many days did Macy record temperatures? _____

3. From the data, what is the season when Macy recorded the temperatures? _____

4. What is the range in temperatures?

_____

5. What is the average temperature?

_____

6. What temperature is the mode?

_____

7. What is the median temperature?

_____

8. On how many days is the temperature 17°? _____

9. How could Macy use the data on this table? _____

_____

10. If a weather forecaster had made this table, how could he or she use the data? _____

_____

✏️ **Answer the questions below.**

11. A local television station polls its viewers on issues in the upcoming election. Viewers call in to vote yes or no. Are the results of these polls representative of all of the television station's viewers? Explain your reasoning.

_____

_____

12. Ray surveys 100 people in a room of 200 and determines that 0.9 of them like to read. Can Ray claim that 90 out of 100 people in the room like to read?

_____

_____

Name _____   Date _____

Say It with Pictures

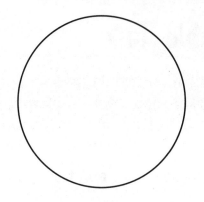

1. A newspaper reported the city's budget as follows: $10,000 for street repairs, $70,000 for building repairs, $120,000 for salaries, and $40,000 for other expenses. Draw a circle graph to show the city's budget.

2. The table shows the number of revolutions per minute (RPM). If the pattern continues, what will be the RPM on speed 5? Show the data in a line graph.

_____

Electric Motor RPM

Speed	RPM
1	125
2	200
3	300
4	450

3. Use the data on the table to make a bar graph.

Favorite Cars

Make of Car	Votes
Ford	21
Chevrolet	15
Plymouth	24
Toyota	12
Honda	18

Name _____ Date _____

Take Your Chance!

 Pick a piece of paper out of a hat.

1. What are the possible outcomes? _____

2. Are they equal outcomes? _____

3. What is the probability that Joan's name is selected? _____

4. What is the probability that a boy's name is selected? _____

5. What is the probability that Thomasin's name is selected? _____

Look at the spinner.
Suppose you spin the arrow 1 time.

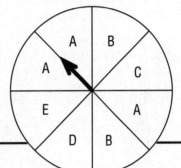

 Write a fraction for each probability.

6. A _____   7. B _____   8. C _____

9. A or D _____   10. A or B _____   11. B or C _____

Andrea is organizing the Parent's Day celebration at school.
She is asked at random to choose one of the following
entertainers: George Fischer, musician; Fanny Andrews,
dancer; Albert Jones, comedian; Susan King, musician.

 Write the probability of each.

12. She will pick a musician. _____

13. She will pick a male entertainer. _____

14. She will pick neither a musician nor a dancer. _____

15. She will pick a magician. _____

Assessment: Probability

Name _____ Date _____

A Whale of a Sight!

A table shows information, or data, so the facts can easily be read and understood.

The table shows data about kinds of whales seen one summer. Use the table to answer the questions below.

Whale Watch Sightings

Kinds of Whale	June	July	August
Humpback	17	4	7
Baleen	4	10	5
Finback	5	9	4
Dolphins	10	12	15

1. In which month were the most baleen whales sighted? _____

2. Were more dolphins or finback whales seen in August? _____

3. How many humpback whales were cited in all? _____

4. In which month were the most whales sighted? _____

5. Make a list of the total number of whales seen in order from least to most.

   _____

   _____

 Extension: Research to find the average lengths of each kind of whale. Make a table to show your data. Then write several questions about your table. Have a classmate answer them.

Name _____ Date _____

Scoring with Tables

Be sure to identify what a question asks you to find.
Then carefully check the facts in the table to find the
correct information.

The table shows outcomes of
games that teams played in a
soccer league. Use the table to
answer the questions below.

Soccer Scores

Team	Wins	Losses	Ties
Tigers	16	4	0
Panthers	9	11	0
Chargers	15	3	2
Thunderbolts	7	11	2
Generals	11	8	1
Cheetahs	6	13	1
Phantoms	10	10	0
Bulldogs	5	15	0
Totals			

1. Which team won as many games as it lost? _____

2. Which team won 2 more games than the Cheetahs lost? _____

3. How many games did the teams play this season? _____

4. Which 2 teams together won as many games as the Generals won?

   _____

5. If all the teams played in a tournament, which team would most likely win?
   Explain your reasoning. _____

   _____

   _____

Extension: Look in the sports section of your newspaper and
find a table. How is the table above like the table you found? How are
they different? _____

   _____

   _____

Name _____ Date _____

They All Fall Down

A table must have a title. Also, all rows and columns have labels.

The list below shows the heights of some waterfalls in the world. Use the list to answer the questions below.

Kukenaam Falls	Venezuela	2,050 feet
Sutherland Falls	New Zealand	1,904 feet
Angel Falls	Venezuela	3,212 feet
Takakkaw Falls	Canada	1,600 feet
Tigela Falls	South Africa	2,800 feet
Wollomombi Falls	Australia	1,580 feet

1. Make a table. Order the names of the falls from least to greatest.

2. Which waterfall is the tallest?

_____

3. Which waterfall is the shortest?

_____

4. Which waterfalls are over 1,900 feet in height? _____

_____

5. Based on the information, what might you conclude about Venezuela? Explain your reasoning.

_____

_____

_____

 Extension: Research to find the names of some waterfalls in the United States. How tall are they? Make a table to show your findings.

Name _____   Date _____

Picture This Table

> You can use a table to make information on a diagram easier to understand.

At Camp Sunfish, the waterfront director made this diagram of the lake to show the swimming classes.

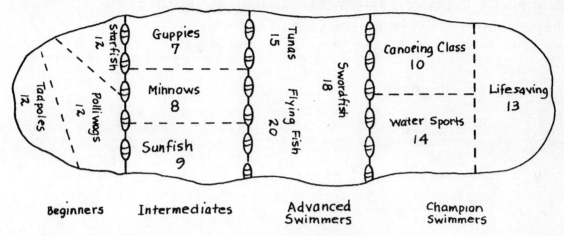

1. Make a table that shows the number of swimmers.

2. How many beginners are there? _____

3. Which group has the most swimmers? _____

4. How many swimmers in all are at the camp? _____

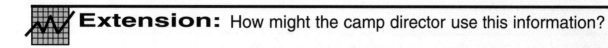

Extension: How might the camp director use this information?

_____

_____

Name _____ Date _____

It's Not Just Bologna!

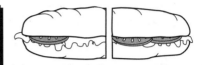

Sometimes a word problem has many facts. Listing the facts in a table can help show how the facts go together.

Shawna works in a sandwich shop. On Monday she sells 23 bologna sandwiches, 57 ham sandwiches, and 36 turkey sandwiches. On Wednesday she sells 19 bologna sandwiches, 46 ham sandwiches, and 20 turkey sandwiches. On Friday she sells 27 bologna sandwiches, 67 ham sandwiches, and 51 turkey sandwiches.

1. Make a table to show the data.

2. How many more turkey sandwiches did Shawna sell on Friday than Monday?

   _____

3. How many bologna sandwiches did Shawna sell in all? _____

4. How many sandwiches did Shawna sell on Friday? _____

5. How could Shawna use this table to help plan for the next week's sales?

   _____

   _____

 Extension: Write your own question about the table. Have a classmate use your table to find the answer. _____

   _____

Name _____   Date _____

Scheduled to Leave

A schedule is a kind of table. It lists the
times something will happen.

Look at this airline schedule.
It lists flights from New York.

New York Flights

Leave New York	Destination	Arrival (New York Time)
8:30 A.M.	St. Louis	12:00 Noon
8:30 A.M.	New Orleans	1:00 P.M.
8:45 A.M.	Atlanta	12:30 P.M.
9:00 A.M.	Miami	3:30 P.M.
10:00 A.M.	Dallas	3:00 P.M.
1:00 P.M.	Phoenix	6:00 P.M.
1:00 P.M.	Denver	5:00 P.M.
1:00 P.M.	Billings	5:15 P.M.
1:15 P.M.	Los Angeles	8:15 P.M.

 Use the schedule to answer the questions below.

1. What time does the flight to Dallas leave? _____

2. How long is the flight to Atlanta? _____

3. Which flights from New York will arrive after 5:00 P.M.? _____

4. Does it take longer to fly to Miami or Los Angeles? _____

5. If it takes 45 minutes to check in for a flight, when should you arrive at the
   airport for a flight to Denver? _____

Extension: Where would you go if you could plan a vacation?
Using an airline or a bus schedule, plan the perfect trip. Include the dates
and times of departures and arrivals.

Name _____   Date _____

Time to Cook

A schedule can help you plan the time
you want to start or finish something.

Dish	How Much	Estimated Cooking Time	Starting Time	Estimated Serving Time
Soup	4 cups			
Beef	5.37 pounds			
Potatoes	4			
Beans	4 cups			
Dessert	6 baked apples			

Manuel is planning a dinner for his friends. He wants to begin dinner
with soup at 5:00 P.M. Use the information below to complete the table.

1. The beef, potatoes, and beans make up the main course and should be served at the same time.

2. Manuel needs to estimate how long it will take to eat the soup so he can figure out when to serve the main course.

3. He needs to estimate how long it will take to eat the main course so he can figure out when to serve the dessert.

4. He allows 30-35 minutes of cooking time for each pound of beef.

5. Baking one potato takes 40 minutes. When baking more than 1 potato, allow at least 5 minutes for each extra potato.

6. The soup should be brought to a boil. Manuel knows it takes 5 minutes for 2 cups of water to boil.

7. The beans are to be cooked in 2 cups of boiling water. Each cup of beans will cook for 2 1/2 minutes.

8. Baking the apples will take 40-45 minutes. They need to cool for 15 minutes.

Extension: Is it better for Manuel to overestimate or underestimate the time? Explain your reasoning.

Name _____   Date _____

What's My Hobby?

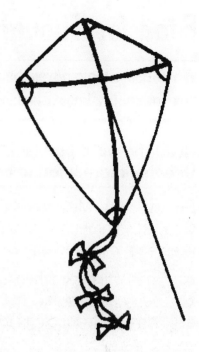

You can use information to solve a problem. A logic table is a quick way to put your information in order.

Jacqueline, Patricia, Louis, and Emanuel like to swim, fly kites, read, and play chess. Each person favors one hobby the most. Find each person's favorite.

a. No person's name has the same number of letters as his or her favorite hobby.

b. The person who likes chess the most is a girl and is friends with both Louis and Patricia.

c. The person who likes reading the most is a boy.

On a logic table, you eliminate a box by putting an X in it, and you can put an O in each box that is correct. For example, Louis's name has the same number of letters as *chess.* Statement **a.** tells you that chess cannot be Louis's favorite.

	Jacqueline	Patricia	Louis	Emanuel
Chess			X	
Reading				
Swimming				
Kite Flying				

 Complete the sentences to tell each friend's favorite hobby.

1. Jacqueline's favorite hobby is

_____ .

2. Patricia's favorite hobby is

_____ .

3. Louis's favorite hobby is

_____ .

4. Emanuel's favorite hobby is

_____ .

Extension: Try writing your own logic problem. Ask a classmate to solve it.

Name _____   Date _____

Food for Thought

When using logic boxes, be sure to write X or O in each box to identify known facts.

 Read the word problem.
Use the information to complete the logic table below. Write _X_ or _O_.

Sherry, Jerry, Merry, and Perry are all friends.
One likes hamburgers, one likes spaghetti, one
likes egg rolls, and one likes tacos.

a. Sherry likes ketchup on her favorite food.
b. Merry always eats her favorite food with a fork.
c. Perry adds toppings to his favorite food.

	Hamburger	Spaghetti	Egg Rolls	Tacos
Sherry				
Jerry				
Merry				
Perry				

 Complete the sentences to tell each friend's favorite food.

1. Sherry likes _____ .

2. Jerry likes _____ .

3. Merry likes _____ .

4. Perry likes _____ .

Extension: Why are these tables called logic tables?

_____

Tables and Data: Using a Logic Table

Tables with Punch

A table can sometimes help you find a
number pattern to solve a problem.

A restaurant has a recipe for punch. The table shows the
amount of each ingredient for the number of people it will serve.

Fruit Punch

2 quarts orange juice

1 1/2 cups unsweetened pineapple juice

4 cups apple juice

Yield: 25 servings

Punch Recipe for a Crowd

Ingredient	25 People	50 People	100 People	200 People
Orange juice	2 quarts	4 quarts		
Pineapple juice	$1\frac{1}{2}$ cups			
Apple juice	1 quart			

 Use the table to answer the questions below.
(HINT: There are 4 quarts in a gallon.)

1. How many gallons of orange juice
   are needed to make punch that
   serves 200 people? _____

2. How many gallons of apple juice are
   needed to make punch that serves
   100 people? _____

3. How many gallons of punch are
   there when the restaurant serves
   200 people? _____

4. The restaurant buys pineapple juice
   in 96 ounce containers. How much
   of 1 container will they use to make
   punch for 100 people? (Hint: There
   are 12 cups in 96 fluid ounces.)

   _____

Extension: Choose a favorite recipe.
Write the recipe to serve 100 people.

Name _____   Date _____

Seed Money

> Many number patterns use multiplication or division.
> A table can make it easier to find the number pattern rule.

✏ **Read the problem. Use the information to make a table.**

The volleyball team is selling seeds to earn money for
new equipment. A packet of seeds sells for $0.50.
Each time the team sells a packet, it earns $0.15.

✏ **Use the table to answer the questions below.**

1. Mr. Miyori buys 3 packets of seeds.
   How much money did the team
   earn? _____

2. How many packets of seeds must
   the team sell to earn $0.75? _____

3. Ena sells 2 packets of seeds to her
   grandmother. She also sells $2.50
   worth of seeds to her teacher. How
   much money did Ena earn for the
   team? _____

4. Dan sells $11.50 in seeds. How
   many packets does he sell?

   _____

5. Mr. Lopez wants to buy enough
   seeds so that the team can buy a
   stopwatch. A stopwatch costs $3.00.
   How many packets of seeds will Mr.
   Lopez buy? _____

 Extension: Many plant nurseries sell plants in packages of 6.
Find out how much different kinds of packaged plants cost. Then make a
number pattern table that shows buying several packages, the number of
plants, and the costs.

Name _____   Date _____

Line Drives

As data is collected, it can be organized on a tally table so it is easy to read. One mark, or tally, stands for 1 item. Every fifth tally mark is a long diagonal slash. You can skip-count by fives to find the total. Frequency is the number total of the tally marks.

The tally table shows the number of runs players on the Super Sonics baseball team scored.

Runs Made by Super Sonics

	Kareem	Delia	Ling	Stacy
Game 1	卌 //	//	卌	/
Game 2	卌	卌	卌	卌
Game 3	卌 卌 卌	卌	/	///

Use the table to answer the questions below.

1. Who scored the most runs for all 3 games? _____

2. How many more runs did the Super Sonics score in game 2 than in game 1? _____

3. In which game did all the players score the same number of runs?

   _____

4. How many runs did the Super Sonics score in all 3 games?

   _____

5. Make a frequency table to show the information on the tally table.

 Extension: Think about the activities you do at school, at home, and during sports events. When could you use a tally table to help you organize data?

Name _____   Date _____

Run for the Tally

Remember, on a tally table:
- Each mark stands for 1 item.
- Every fifth tally mark is a long diagonal slash.
- You can skip-count by fives to find the frequency.

The list below shows the time it takes for each member on a track team to run the 40-yard dash.

10.1	11.3	12.4	9.4	7.2	8.1	7.5	10.5	12.3
11.1	12.1	10.4	8.8	9.2	13.2	8.4	10.3	12.1
11.6	9.6	8.9	9.9	10.4	9.4	7.9	8.5	10.5
12.1	9.8	8.8	8.9	10.4	13.2	9.9	10.1	11.1

 Answer the questions below.

1. On your tally sheet, will you write each time or group the times, for example, grouping all ties from 8 to 10 seconds? Explain your reasoning.

   _____

   _____

2. Will you use decimals or whole numbers for the times on your tally sheet? Explain your reasoning.

   _____

   _____

3. Will the total number of runners who ran the race in 8 to 10 seconds be easier to find on the tally sheet or the frequency table?

   _____

4. What will be the fastest time shown on your tally sheet?

   _____

5. Make a tally sheet and frequency table.

 Extension: Use the tables above to write questions. Have a classmate solve them.

Name _____   Date _____

Going to School

| One table can be made to show both tally marks and frequency. |

Most of the sixth-grade class live on Bank Street, Mill Street, or Front Street. The students have different ways to get to school.

Jack–Bank St., bike	Jim–Mill St., bike	Michael–Mill St., bus
Marcia–Mill St., walk	Kelly–Front St., car	Danny–Bank St., bike
George–Front St., bike	Joe–Mill St., bike	Julio–Front St., car
Fred–Bank St., car	Elena–Bank St., car	David–Mill St., bus
Susan–Mill St., walk	Tara–Front St., walk	Agnes–Bank St., bike
Jane–Front St., bus	Samuel–Mill St., bus	Chris–Front St., car

 Answer the questions below.

1. Make a tally and frequency table to show how the students get to school.

3. How could the data in exercise 1 be used by people in the school?

   _____

   _____

4. How could the data in exercise 2 be used by people in the school?

   _____

   _____

2. Make a tally and frequency table to show where the students live.

 Extension: Make a tally table to show how your classmates get to school. What conclusions can you make based on the data?

Tables and Data: Making a Tally Table

Name _____   Date _____

Eggs-tra Easy Samples

When you analyze a group of things, it is sometimes more practical to look at a small section of the group. This is called a sampling. In order for the data to be accurate, the sample group should be as similar as possible to the group as a whole.

Albert has just taken a job as an egg spot-checker. Albert must check 2 cartons out of every 100 that the company ships to stores. He checks for cracked eggs, empty egg pockets, and other problems.

 Answer the questions below.

1. On Monday Albert checks 2 cartons from the top of every crate of 100. Is his sampling accurate? Explain your reasoning. _____

   _____

2. On Tuesday Albert checks 200 of the 10,000 cartons that are shipped. He finds 10 with broken eggs in them. He reports that only 10 imperfect cartons were shipped. Is his report correct? Explain your reasoning.

   _____

   _____

3. On Wednesday, Albert accidentally drops a crate of eggs. When he opens the first carton from the crate, half of the eggs are broken. So are half of the eggs in the second carton. He reports that half of the eggs shipped that day were broken. Is this accurate? Explain your reasoning. _____

   _____

4. On Friday, Albert checks 100 cartons out of 5,000. He finds only one broken egg. He reports 50 broken eggs in 5,000 cartons. Is his report accurate? Explain your reasoning.

   _____

   _____

Extension: How could Albert's checking procedure be changed so as to more accurately reflect the number of irregularities found by the customer?

_____

_____

Name _____   Date _____

Soup-er Samples

A survey asks a group of people their opinion about a topic. It is impossible to ask everyone, so samples, a small group of people, are used. From a sample, a prediction of likes and dislikes can be made. The larger the group, the more accurate the results of the survey will be.

Souper Soup Company thinks that its new carrot soup will be very popular. The company took a survey of its employees to see what people thought about the soup.

 Answer the questions below.

1. Souper Soup surveyed 4 of the 5,000 employees. All 4 loved the soup. The company said that everyone loved the soup. Was this a good sample? Explain your reasoning. _____

_____

2. Next, the company surveyed 1,000 of its employees, and 900 said they loved the soup. The company decided that 9 out of every 10 people would love the soup. Was this a good sample? Explain your reasoning. _____

_____

3. Souper Soup surveyed 1,000 employees of the Simmering Soup Company, a rival soup maker. New carrot soup was not a hit. Only 25 people liked it. What was wrong with this sample? _____

_____

4. What would be a good sample group for Souper Soup to test its new carrot soup? _____

_____

Extension: If you had to find the favorite song of the people at your school, how would you set up a sample group? Who should be sampled and how many would you survey? _____

_____

_____

Name _____   Date _____

What Does It Mean?

A survey cannot ask a large group of people their opinion. Instead, the data collected from the sample group is used to predict what a larger group will think.

A sample can be random, meaning there is no real order to the choosing of the people. Or the sample can be scientific, meaning the poll asks representative people.

For example, you want to conduct a lunchroom poll about favorite foods. You could use a random sample, where you ask every third or fourth student what he or she likes to eat. Or you could use a scientific sample, where you ask an even number of boys and girls.

You decide to ask 20 girls and 20 boys in the sixth grade what their favorite food is. You put the results on a table.

Food	Girls	Boys
Pizza	7	8
Hamburger	5	4
Taco	5	6
Hot Dog	3	2

 Use the table to answer the questions below.

1. If 7 out of 20 girls like pizza, how many girls out of 100 would probably like pizza? _____

2. If 6 out of 20 boys like tacos, how many boys out of 200 would probably like tacos? _____

3. If 5 out of 40 boys and girls like hot dogs, how many boys and girls out of 120 would probably like hot dogs?

   _____

4. If 20 out of 40 boys and girls like hamburgers and tacos, how many boys and girls out of 400 would probably like hamburgers and tacos?

   _____

Extension: Repeat the survey above, asking 20 boys and 20 girls to name their favorite food. How does your data compare with the table above?

Name _____   Date _____

Questionable Music

A survey asks a group of people their opinion about a topic. You can use a tally table to help you keep track of the answers, or votes. Use 1 tally mark for each answer.

Take a survey. Ask at least 20 students in your classroom what their favorite kind of music is. Organize the data on a tally table.

Favorite Music

Music	Tally	Frequency
Classical		
Country		
Jazz		
Rap		
Rock		
Other		

Use your tally table to answer the questions below.

1. Which music is liked by the greatest number of students?

   _____

2. Which music do the least number of students like?

   _____

3. What is the difference between the number of people who like rap best and the number who like country best?

   _____

4. What conclusions can you draw from this data?

   _____

   _____

5. Could you use this data to predict the kind of music favored by all the students in the school?

   _____

 Extension: Each week, radio stations and newspapers list the top ten albums and singles for the week. How do you think they collect this data?

I Want to Know!

When taking a survey, you will need to:
- Choose the question.
- Decide on the sample group.
- Collect the data.
- Make conclusions based on the data.

What kind of survey would you like to take? Plan how you will conduct the survey. Make a table to collect your data.

Write a paragraph to tell what you found out through your survey.

_____

_____

_____

_____

_____

 Extension: Think about your survey. Do you think your sampling was accurate? How could you have improved it so that the data would be more representative of the group?

Name _____   Date _____

What Do You Mean?

You can find the average, or mean, of a set of numbers by adding all of the numbers and dividing the sum by the number of addends.

For the month of March, Maya kept a record of 4 types of books borrowed from the library. She wants to figure out the average number of books taken out during Week 1. To find the average, Maya uses these steps:

- She adds all of the books taken out of the library the first week.
- Then she divides the sum by the total number of book categories.

The average number of books borrowed from the library in the first week was 26.

Library Books Borrowed in March

Week	Adventure	Travel	Biography	Children's Books
1	30	30	19	25
2	24	18	23	32
3	20	21	33	22
4	22	23	17	25

 Use the table to answer the questions below.

1. What was the average number of travel books taken out in these 4 weeks? _____

2. Which type of book averaged more take-outs in the 4 weeks, adventure or children's books?

    _____

3. Which type of book averaged the most take-outs for this 4-week period? _____

4. Which week averaged the most take-outs? _____

Extension: Find ways that averages are used at school and home.

Name _____   Date _____

They Play Mean!

Remember, to find the average, or mean, of a set of numbers, add all of the numbers and divide the sum by the number of addends.

In baseball, a player's batting average is the number of times the player hit the ball safely divided by the number of times the player tried to hit the ball. The number is represented in thousands for greater accuracy. For example, when a batter has 50 attempts (at-bats) and gets 17 hits, the player's average is 17/50, or .340.

 Answer the questions below.

1. When a batter has 12 hits in 50 at-bats, what is the batter's batting average? _____

2. If a batter has an average of .420 after 50 at-bats, how may balls did the player hit? _____

3. The same batter's average drops to .400 after 25 more at-bats. How many balls out of the 25 did the batter hit? _____

4. How many balls out of the 75 at-bats did the player miss? _____

There are a few players who can hit the ball from both right-handed and left-handed stances. These batters are called switch-hitters. Switch-hitters keep averages for both sides to see from which side they bat better. A batter might hit 30% left-handed and 35% right-handed. The player's total batting average is $\frac{.300 + .350}{2}$, or .325.

5. A switch-hitter is batting .320 right-handed after 50 at-bats. The batter hits 20 out of 50 balls hitting left-handed. What is the total batting average? _____

Extension: Why do teams keep data on the scores of individual players as well as on the team? How do people use this information?

Name _____   Date _____

Tennis Is the Mode

> The mode is the number that occurs the most often in a set of numbers.

Don is a member of the Net Set Tennis Club.
He makes a table to show the age of each member
and the number of years each person has played.

The Net Set Tennis Club

Name	Years Played	Age	Name	Years Played	Age
Lee	4	14	Keisha	1	9
Mark	2	13	Don	5	12
Lynn	5	12	Daniel	2	14
Terri	1	9	Sherry	3	10
Melissa	4	14	Jim	5	13
Greg	5	12	Luis	3	12

 Use the table to answer the questions below.

1. Write all the ages of the tennis players from the greatest to the least. _____

   _____

2. Which number occurs most often?

   _____

3. Write all the years the members have played from the least to the greatest. _____

   _____

4. Which number occurs most often?

   _____

5. When could knowing the mode of a set of numbers be useful to people who keep data? _____

   _____

Extension: Are you a member of a club? Make a table showing the ages and the years that each member has been involved in that activity. Find the mode of each. What does the information tell you?

Name _____ Date _____

Trash in the Median

To find the median number, order a set of numbers from the least to greatest. The middle number is the median number. If there is an even amount of numbers, then you find the mean of the middle two numbers.

The table shows the recycling materials and their weights that the students in Mr. Ito's class collected in five weeks.

Weight of Recycling Materials

	Week 1	Week 2	Week 3	Week 4	Week 5
Cans	45 lb.	42 lb.	60 lb.	60 lb.	50 lb.
Glass	55 lb.	42 lb.	28 lb.	35 lb.	38 lb.
Newspaper	67 lb.	59 lb.	70 lb.	62 lb.	65 lb.
Plastic	21 lb.	13 lb.	11 lb.	19 lb.	9 lb.

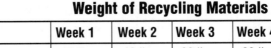

 Use the table to answer the questions below.

1. Write all the weights of the recyclable materials collected during week 3 from the least to the greatest. What is the median number? _____

   _____

2. What is the median number for the weight of all of the materials collected in week 1?

   _____

3. What is the median number for the weight of all of the plastic collected?

   _____

4. What is the median number for the weight of all of the cans collected?

   _____

5. How could data about the median weight be used by a recycling company? _____

   _____

   _____

 Extension: If a teacher listed the grades of a test for the whole class, why would knowing the mean, mode, and median of the scores be helpful?

_____

Name _____   Date _____

The Camera's Range

The range is the difference between the least number and the greatest number in a set of numbers.

The picture shows the camera equipment on display at the Shutterbug Camera Shop.

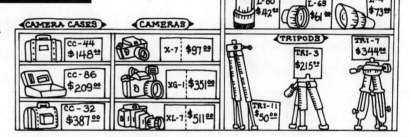

 Use the picture to answer the questions below.

1. What is the range in prices for tripods? _____

2. What is the range in prices for cameras? _____

3. What is the range in prices for lenses? _____

4. What is the range in prices for camera cases? _____

5. Suppose you set a range to spend between $300 to $350 on camera equipment. Which equipment will you buy? _____

_____

6. Suppose you want to spend between $600 to $700 to buy camera equipment. You are going to buy a camera, lens, tripod, and case. Which kind of each equipment will you buy? _____

_____

Extension: How would knowing the range of prices in products at different stores make you a smart consumer? _____

_____

_____

Name _____ Date _____

These Pictures Count!

Graphs are pictures showing information. A pictograph is one kind of graph. It uses pictures to show data. Each picture stands for a certain number of people or things.

Westwood School held its student council election. The pictograph shows the results of the election.

Results of Student Council Election

Person	Number of Votes
Fran	☐ ☐ ☐ ☐ ☐ ☐ ☐
Ben	☐ ☐ ☐ ☐ ☐ ☐
Crissy	☐ ☐ ☐ ☐ ☐ ☐ ☐ ☐ ☐
Anil	☐ ☐ ☐ ☐ ☐ ☐
Angelina	☐ ☐ ☐ ☐

☐ = 10 votes

 Use the pictograph to answer the questions below.

1. How many votes does each symbol stand for?

   _____

2. Which 2 students got the same number of votes?

   _____

3. Who won the election?

   _____

4. How many votes did Fran get?

   _____

5. According to the pictograph, how many students voted?

   _____

6. In making this pictograph, how might estimation be used? Explain your reasoning. _____

   _____

   _____

Extension: Look in newspapers and magazines for pictographs. How are they the same? How are they different?

Name _____   Date _____

Weather or Not

In a pictograph, each symbol stands for a certain number of people or things. When part of a symbol is shown, it stands for a smaller number.

Look at the pictograph for the average daily hours of sunlight in Alaska. It shows the average hours of sunlight for days in spring, summer, fall, and winter.

Average Daily Hours of Sunlight in Alaska

Spring	⬡ ⬡ ⬡ ⬡ ◖
Summer	⬡ ⬡ ⬡ ⬡ ⬡ ⬡ ⬡ ⬡ ⬡ ◕
Fall	⬡ ⬡ ⬡ ⬡ ◿
Winter	⬡ ◿

⬡ = 2 hours

Use the pictograph to answer the questions below.

1. How many hours does each symbol stand for?

   ⬡ = _____   ◕ = _____

   ◖ = _____   ◿ = _____

2. How many hours of sunlight are there on a day in spring? in winter? _____

3. How many more hours of sunlight are there on a summer day than on a spring day? _____

4. How many more hours of darkness than sunlight are there on a fall day? _____

5. How many more hours of darkness are there on a winter day than on a fall day? _____

6. When would you like to visit Alaska? Explain your reasoning. _____

   _____

 Extension: Make a table to show the hours of darkness for Alaska. Then show the data in a pictograph.

Name _____   Date _____

Industrial Strength Graphs

Remember:
- a pictograph has a title and a picture key.
- each picture key stands for a certain number of people or things.
- part of a symbol in a pictograph stands for a smaller number.

The table below shows the leading automobile-manufacturing states in 1981. Complete the table by rounding each number to the nearest hundred thousand.

Cars Manufactured

State	Number	Rounded Number
Michigan	2,031,000	
Delaware	531,000	
Missouri	524,000	
Georgia	481,000	
Illinois	403,000	
New Jersey	374,000	
Oklahoma	329,000	
Wisconsin	322,000	

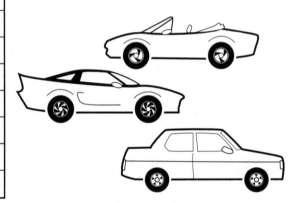

Make a pictograph to show the number of cars manufactured. Each picture key should stand for 100,000 cars.

_____

Extension: Which manufacturing industries are of economic importance to your state? Make a pictograph showing the income produced from the top 5 industries.

Name _____ Date _____

Booked Up

When comparing pictographs, check both picture keys to find out how many each symbol stands for. Then carefully count totals in each category before comparing.

Two bookstores record data for the books they sell in the month of June.

Book Nook June Sales

Kind of Books	Books Sold
Adventure	📖 📖 📖 📖
Mystery	📖 📖 📖
Fantasy	📖 📖 📖 📖 📖
Nonfiction	📖 📖
Other	📖 📖

📖 = 100 books

Reading Room June Sales

Kind of Books	Books Sold
Mystery	📖 📖 📖 📖
Fantasy	📖 📖 📖 📖 📖
Adventure	📖 📖 📖 📖 📖 📖 📖
Jokes/Riddles	📖
Other	📖 📖

📖 = 50 books

 Use the pictographs to answer the questions below.

1. Which store sold nonfiction books? How many books did it sell?

_____

2. Which store sold more mystery books? How many more books did it sell? _____

_____

3. Which kind of books did the Reading Room sell the most of?

_____

4. Which kind of books did the stores sell the same number of?

_____

5. How many books did the Book Nook sell in June?

_____

6. How could the manager of the Reading Room use this data?

_____

 Extension: Make a pictograph showing the kinds of books a family member owns. Compare your pictograph to a classmate's pictograph. What can you tell by comparing the graphs?

Name _____   Date _____

Going to New Heights

A bar graph uses bars to show information. The bars can be vertical or horizontal. The heights or lengths of the bars make it easier to compare data.

A vertical bar graph is shown here. The title tells you what it is about. To read it, put your finger on a year at the bottom of the graph. Move your finger to the top of the bar that stands for that year. Now move your finger left to the scale. The number there tells you the number of immigrants entering the United States for that year.

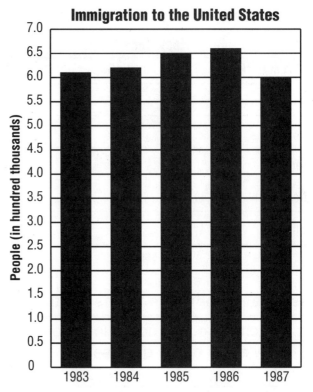

Immigration to the United States

People (in hundred thousands)

 Use the graph to answer the questions below.

1. Which year did the greatest number of immigrants enter the United States? _____

2. Which year did about 650,000 people immigrate? _____

3. Which year did the number of people immigrating to the United States decrease? _____

4. How does the graph make it easier to tell whether there were more people immigrating into the United States in 1983 or 1985? _____
_____

Extension: Research to find the number of immigrants entering the United States in the last 3 years. How has the data changed from what this graph presents?

Name _____   Date _____

City Shirt Sales

Bar graphs have titles, a scale to show amounts, and a category to tell which items are being compared.

This graph is a horizontal bar graph. The bars run left to right. It shows the number of shirts the Sanchez Shirt Stores sell in 5 cities. To read a horizontal bar graph, put your finger on the name of a city. Move your finger right to the end of the bar for that city. Now move your finger down to the scale at the bottom of the graph. The number tells you the number of shirts sold in that city.

Sanchez Shirt Sales in 1998

Number of Shirts (in thousands)

 Use the graph to answer the questions below.

1. How many shirts were sold in Reno?

   _____

2. Which city sold 3,000 shirts?

   _____

3. Which store will get the award for the most sales? _____

4. The owner of all 4 stores wanted to sell 21,000 shirts in 1998. Did the owner meet the goal? Explain your reasoning. _____

   _____

5. If shirts cost $11 each, how much money did the store in Boston earn?

   _____

6. When looking at this graph, what information might the owner consider to determine why sales are so different? _____

   _____

   _____

 Extension: Look in newspapers and magazines for bar graphs. Are they vertical or horizontal? How are they alike? How are they different?

Name _____ Date _____

Breezy Bars

Remember, a bar graph compares data by using different lengths or heights of bars. If bars end between numbers on the scale, you will have to estimate the number of items in that category.

The table shows the maximum wind speeds clocked at weather stations in several cities.

Maximum Wind Speeds

Station	Speed (in MPH)
Atlanta, GA	70
Bismarck, ND	72
Cape Hatteras, NC	110
Denver, CO	56
Fort Smith, AR	58
Galveston, TX	100

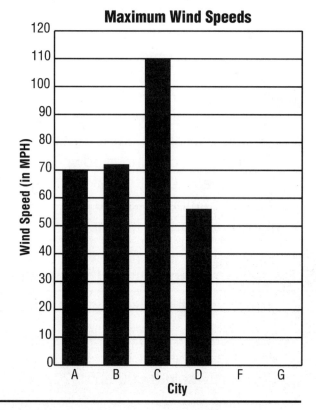

Maximum Wind Speeds

 Answer the questions below.

1. Use the table to show the bars for Fort Smith and Galveston.

2. Which city had the greatest wind speed? _____

3. What is the range of the wind speeds listed on the table?

_____

4. From this graph, can you determine which city is the windiest? Explain your reasoning. _____

_____

_____

Extension: Research to find the maximum wind speeds for cities in your state. Make a bar graph to show the data.

Name _____ Date _____

The Best Sales—Bar None

Remember, a bar graph compares data. Check the scale carefully to see the number values, such as tens, hundreds, or millions.

The table shows the number of televisions a manufacturing company shipped.

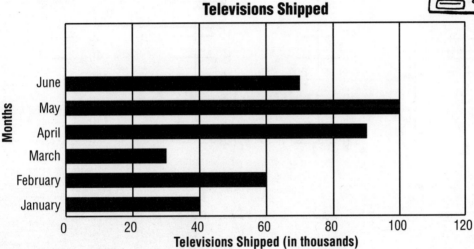

Televisions Shipped

Months: June, May, April, March, February, January

Televisions Shipped (in thousands): 0, 20, 40, 60, 80, 100, 120

 Answer the questions below.

1. What scale is shown on the graph?

   _____

2. Were more televisions sold in January or March?

   _____

3. How many televisions were sold in June? _____

4. The company shipped 48,000 televisions in July and 82,000 in August. Show this information on the graph.

Extension: Look in the newspaper for an advertisement showing televisions. Choose one model and write the price. What would have been the potential earnings of the manufacturing company if they had sold all of the televisions for the price you listed?

Name _____ Date _____

Scaled to Size

The scale of the graph is the measurement of items. It is made up of units that are equal in number. When the data numbers are large, generally, the scale intervals will be large, too.

 Write the letter of the most reasonable scale for each set of data.

1.

Favorite Subjects

Subject	Number of Students
Reading	10
Mathematics	15
Language	12
Science	25
History	10

a.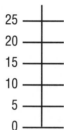

b.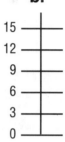

c.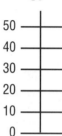

_____

2.

Favorite Sports

Sport	Number of Students
Baseball	50
Soccer	90
Basketball	70
Bowling	20
Tennis	15

a.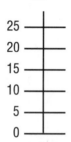

b.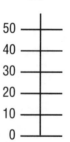

c.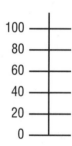

_____

 Look at the table. Write the scale you would use to make a graph for this data.

3.

Favorite Music

Music	Number of Students
Rap	450
Country	200
Jazz	150
Rock	350
Classical	100

 Extension: Look in your science and social studies books for examples of bar graphs. How many numbers are generally listed on the scale? Can you find a pattern that helps you decide how to choose a scale?

Graphs: Understanding Scale

Statistics and Probability 5-6, SV 7479-0

Name _____   Date _____

Taking Attendance

To make a graph, remember to:
- choose a scale.
- label the graph categories.
- give the graph a title.

The table shows the attendance at a high-school football game.

High-School Football Attendance

Week	Number of People
Week 1	395
Week 2	305
Week 3	295
Week 4	450

 Use the list to answer the questions below.

1. Make a vertical bar graph to show the information.
   (HINT: The scale should run up the left side of the graph.)

2. Which week had the largest attendance? _____

3. Which weeks had about the same attendance? _____

4. What was the average attendance for the 4 weeks? _____

 Extension: Find the names of the stadiums in which the last 5 Super Bowl games were played. What was the attendance at these games? Make a table and vertical bar graph to show the data.

Graphs: Making a Vertical Bar Graph

Name _____   Date _____

Animals Behind the Bars

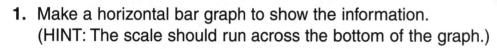

Sometimes a bar graph can help organize data in a word problem. It will make the problem easier to understand.

Marcus surveyed the students in the school to find out what their favorite endangered animal was. There were 61 students who said bald eagles, 92 who said manatees, 45 who said snow leopards, and 76 who said pandas.

1. Make a horizontal bar graph to show the information.
   (HINT: The scale should run across the bottom of the graph.)

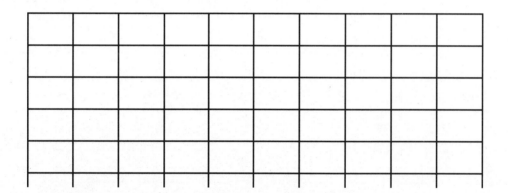

 Use your horizontal bar graph to answer the questions below.

2. Did more students choose pandas or snow leopards?

   _____

3. How many classmates said manatees and bald eagles?

   _____

4. How many people did Marcus survey?

   _____

5. The students in Marcus's class want to sponsor an endangered animal. Which animal do you think they will sponsor? Explain your reasoning.

   _____

   _____

Extension: Several animals are endangered, which means there are few of them left. Research to find 5 kinds of animals that are endangered and how many of them are left. Then make a horizontal bar graph to show your results.

Graphs: Making a Horizontal Bar Graph

Name _____ Date _____

The Coolest Flavors

A survey asks a group of people their opinion about a topic. The information is collected on a table. Then it can be shown on a bar graph so you can see how the data compares.

Take a survey. Ask your classmates to tell their favorite ice-cream flavor. Make a table to organize the information. Then show the data on a bar graph.

 Use your bar graph to answer the questions below.

1. How many people did you poll?

_____

2. Do you think the people you asked were a good sample? Explain your reasoning. _____

_____

3. Do more people prefer vanilla or chocolate? _____

4. Which flavor had the least votes?

_____

Extension: How could the cafeteria use this information?

Name _____ Date _____

Double Up on the News

Double-bar graphs are used to compare two sets of information that cover the same period of time.

When the student councils at Pine Ridge School and Marble Creek School had a 4-week newspaper drive, they used a double graph to show the number of pounds of paper they collected each week.

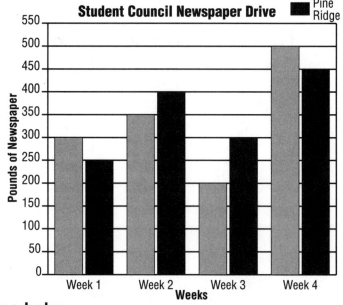

Student Council Newspaper Drive

Legend:
- Marble Creek (gray)
- Pine Ridge (black)

Y-axis: Pounds of Newspaper (0 to 550)
X-axis: Weeks (Week 1, Week 2, Week 3, Week 4)

Use the graph to answer the questions below.

1. How many pounds of newspaper were collected by both groups in Week 1? _____

2. Which group collected more pounds of newspaper in Week 2?

   _____

3. How many more pounds of newspaper were collected by the Marble Creek student council in Week 4? _____

4. How many pounds of newspaper were collected by the Pine Ridge student council? _____

5. The principals of both schools said that the students could take a picnic to the park if they collected over 1,000 pounds of newspapers. Will either school be able to go? If so, which school(s)? _____

   _____

6. The recycling company pays $0.05 per pound of newspaper. How much did each school earn? _____

   _____

   _____

 Extension: Weigh a week's worth of newspaper. How many pounds of newspaper could be recycled each month? each year? Calculate how many pounds could be recycled by the class for each time period.

Graphs: Reading a Double-Bar Graph

Name _____ Date _____

The Temperature's Rising!

Line graphs are used to show how data changes over time. A trend in data is the direction that the recorded information takes, usually developing a pattern to indicate what might happen in the near future.

This line graph shows the recorded temperatures one morning for a city in Greenland. To read it, put your finger on the bottom of the graph. Move your finger up to the dot for that time. Then move your finger to the left to find the temperature.

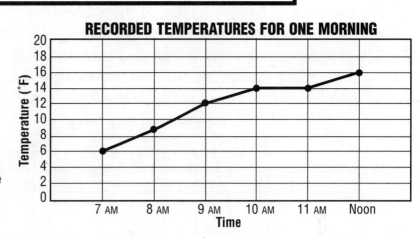

RECORDED TEMPERATURES FOR ONE MORNING

Temperature (°F) / Time: 7 AM, 8 AM, 9 AM, 10 AM, 11 AM, Noon

✏️ **Use the graph to answer the questions below.**

1. At which time was the highest temperature recorded?

   _____

2. At which times were the same temperature recorded?

   _____

3. What is the range in temperature readings? _____

4. If the trend continues, what will the temperature be at 2:00 P.M.? Explain your reasoning. _____

   _____

   _____

GREENLAND

 Extension: Record the temperature every hour for one morning. Do you see a trend in the rise of the temperature? What does the data tell you?

Graphs: Reading a Line Graph

Statistics and Probability 5-6, SV 7479-0

Name _____   Date _____

The Ups and Downs of Movies

To understand a line graph:
- Read the title to understand what information is be shown.
- Know what time period is being shown across the bottom of the graph.
- Know the scale to find the number of items being compared.

The Roxy movie theater has 250 seats. Attendance at the theater varies from night to night. Sometimes it is full. Sometimes only 100 seats are sold. In one 2-week period, the manager made a line graph of attendance.

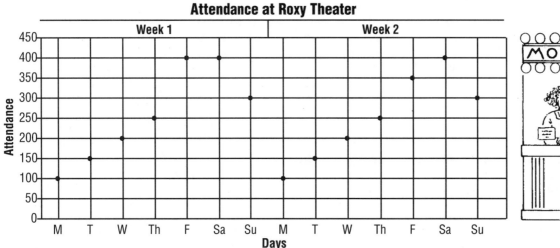

Use the graph to answer the questions below.

1. Draw the lines to complete the line graph.

2. On which night did attendance increase most from the night before?

3. How many more tickets were sold on the first Sunday than on the second Sunday? _____

4. The manager decides not to work on the slowest days of the week. Which 2 days will she not work?

   _____

5. If the trend continues, which nights will be the busiest at the Roxy Theater? Why are these nights the busiest? Explain your reasoning.

   _____

   _____

   _____

 Extension: Look in your social studies book to find other examples of line graphs. Write a list of questions that can be answered by the graph. Have a classmate answer the questions.

The Ticket Line

Remember, a line graph must have:
- a title.
- a scale along the side of the graph.
- the time period across the bottom of the graph.
- both categories labeled with the data being shown.

The table shows the number of raffle
tickets sold over a 5-month period.

Raffle Ticket Sales

Month	Number Sold
July	200
August	180
September	150
October	170
November	200

 Answer the questions below.

1. If you made a line graph of the data, what intervals would you use on the vertical scale?

   _____

2. What would you title the graph?

   _____

3. Which labels would you write for the scale and data category?

   _____

4. Use the data in the table to make a line graph.

Extension: Write some questions about the graph. Ask a classmate to answer them.

Name _____ Date _____

On-Line for Business

You can use a line graph to help solve word problems. First, make a table of the information, then record the data on a graph. If the points of the line graph are between numbers of the scale, you will need to estimate the number of items.

Photolink, Inc., sells photographs of exotic places around the world to newspapers, magazines, and publishers. Yearly sales are divided into quarters. For 1998 they recorded that first-quarter sales amounted to 900 photos. The second-quarter sales amounted to 960, and third-quarter sales amounted to 870 photographs. Fourth-quarter sales were $\frac{1}{3}$ greater than were first-quarter sales.

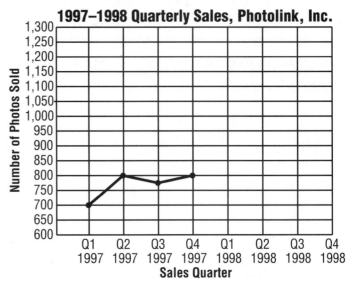

✏ **Answer the questions below.**

1. Make a table to show the data for Photolink's 1998 quarterly sales.

2. Use the table to complete the line graph.

3. What was the general trend for Photolink, Inc.?

    _____

    _____

4. What was the average number of photos sold per quarter in 1998?

    _____

    _____

    _____

 Extension: Look in the business section of the newspaper to find examples of line graphs. What other types of data do companies record on line graphs? How are the graphs alike? How are they different?

Name _____   Date _____

Doubling Up

Double-line graphs are often used to compare information for different years. The different years can be shown by using solid lines and dotted lines or lines that are different colors.

Westech is a producer of microcomputers and computer software. To help them plan production for 1999, a broken-line graph was drawn to illustrate the company's production levels for 1997 and 1998. Each of the levels for 1998 was $3\frac{1}{2}$ times greater per quarter than the 1997 levels of software production for the same quarter. Computer production was $\frac{7}{8}$ of the 1997 levels for each quarter.

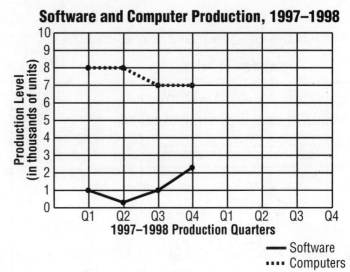

Software and Computer Production, 1997–1998

Production Level (in thousands of units)

1997–1998 Production Quarters

—— Software
•••• Computers

 Use the graph to answer the questions below.

1. Use the information to graph the data for the 1998 production.

_____

2. What was the trend for 1998 software production levels?

_____

3. What was the trend for the 1997 computer production levels?

_____

4. For the first quarter of 1999, Westech wanted their software production to be at least twice the first-quarter production level of 1998. Do they need to increase current production levels? If so, by how much?

_____

_____

_____

Extension: Look in the business section of the newspaper. Choose 1 stock you would like to buy. Follow the market for that stock each day for a week, making a line graph to record its activity. What do you think the trend for this stock will be next week?

Name _____   Date _____

A Double Dose of Rain

When making graphs, it may be necessary to round numbers so it is easier to plot them. Also, you may need to estimate where to place points on a graph.

1. The table shows the rainfall in Tulsa.
Use the data to make a line graph.

Rainfall in Tulsa

Month	Rain (in inches)
March	14.2
April	12.4
May	10.6
June	1.1
July	2.3

2. Make a double-line graph. Use a different color to display the data below on the graph you made for Exercise 1. Revise the labels on your graph.
(HINT: Don't forget the key.)

Rainfall in Columbia

Month	Rain (in inches)
March	12.3
April	10.2
May	9.5
June	4.2
July	3.1

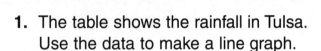 **Extension:** From the double-line graph above, what comparisons can you make about the weather in Tulsa and Columbia?

_____

_____

Name _____   Date _____

Come into the Circle

A circle graph looks just like it sounds. Each slice of the circle is a piece of information included in the circle. The size of each piece shows its relationship to the whole and to each other piece of the circle.

Rita conducted a survey of students at Jacksonville Intermediate School to find out what after-school activities they participated in. The circle graph shows the results.

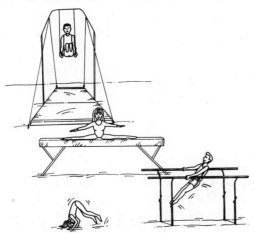

After-School Activities

Hobbies
10

Television Viewing
10

Sports
20

 Use the circle graph to answer the questions below.

1. What is the title of this graph?

_____

2. How is each part labeled?

_____

3. How many students were surveyed?

_____

4. What fractional part of the students have hobbies as an after-school activity? _____

5. How does the part of the class that prefers television viewing compare to the part that prefers sports?

_____

6. How would Rita change the graph if the same number of students liked each choice? _____

_____

Extension: Look in your social studies book for other examples of circle graphs. How are they the same? How are they different?

Name _____   Date _____

Animals in the Circle of Life

Sometimes a circle graph uses percentages to show data.
The sum of the pieces of the circle is 1, or 100%.
The larger the part, the larger the percentage is.

Animals at the Colorado Canyon Institute
(700 animals in all)

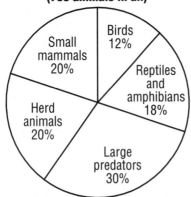

Small mammals 20%
Birds 12%
Reptiles and amphibians 18%
Herd animals 20%
Large predators 30%

Endangered Species
(140 animals in all)

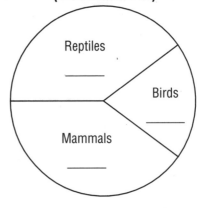

Reptiles
_____
Birds
_____
Mammals
_____

Use the circle graphs to answer the questions below.

1. How many reptiles and amphibians are there at the zoo?

   _____

2. Of the herd of animals at the zoo, 36 are gazelles. How many of the herd animals are not gazelles?

   _____

3. How many more herd animals are there than reptiles and amphibians?

   _____

4. There are 28 birds in the endangered species section at the zoo. What percent is this? Write the percent on the graph.

   _____

5. What is the percentage of endangered reptiles at the zoo? Write the percent on the graph.

   _____

6. What is the percentage of endangered mammals at the zoo? Write the percent on the graph.

   _____

 Extension: Use a calculator to find the number of animals in each category.

Name _____ Date _____

Summer Fun

> Sometimes a circle graph uses fractions to show data.
> The sum of the fractional pieces must equal 1.

This circle graph shows how Keisha spent her summer.

Keisha's Summer Activities

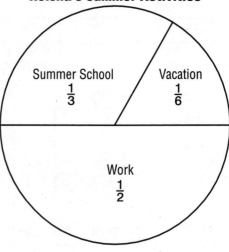

Summer School $\frac{1}{3}$

Vacation $\frac{1}{6}$

Work $\frac{1}{2}$

 Use the circle graph to answer the questions below.

1. Did Keisha spend more time on vacation or at summer school?

   _____

2. What did Keisha spend most of her time doing? _____

3. Make a table to show how you spend your time during a typical summer day.

   Summer Day Activities

Activity	Number of Hours

4. Use the table you made in Exercise 3 to make a circle graph to display the data about your summer activities. (HINT: Don't forget to label your graph.)

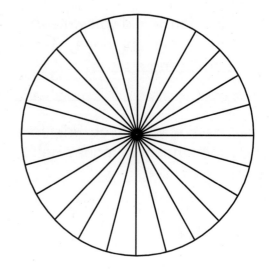

 Extension: Write questions based on the data in your graph. Ask a classmate to answer the questions.

Name _____ Date _____

An Expense Statement!

You can make a circle graph using data in a table. Each piece of data is a piece in the circle graph. First find the sum of all the pieces. Then find the fraction of each piece by using the data as the numerator and the total as the denominator.

The table shows how Beth spends the money she earned while baby-sitting.

Beth's Expenditures

Movie	$5
Clothes	$25
CDs	$10
Savings	$20

 Use the table to answer the questions below.

1. How much did Beth earn while baby-sitting?

   _____

2. What fraction would you write to show the amount of money Beth spent on going to a movie?

   _____

3. What fraction would you write to show the amount of money Beth spent on buying clothes?

   _____

4. What fraction would you write to show the amount of money Beth spent on CDs? _____

5. What fraction would you write to show the amount of money Beth saved? _____

6. Color the circle graph to show how Beth spends her baby-sitting money. (HINT: Don't forget to label the graph.)

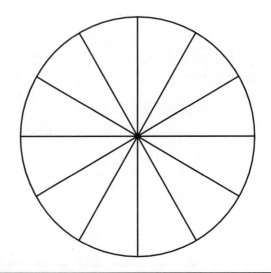

 Extension: Make a circle graph to show how you would spend $100.

Graphs: Making a Circle Graph

Statistics and Probability 5-6, SV 7479-0

Name _____ Date _____

It's Only a Proposal

When comparing circle graphs, make sure you are comparing the same two items.

The Camera Club made a budget for their proposed expenditures for 1998 and showed the data in a circle graph. At the end of the year, the club made a second graph to show how much they actually spent.

Proposed 1998 Budget

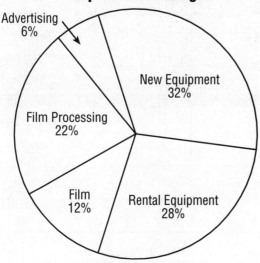

Advertising
6%
Film Processing
22%
New Equipment
32%
Film
12%
Rental Equipment
28%

Total Budget: $8,450

Actual 1998 Budget

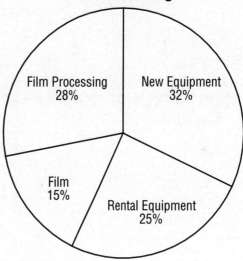

Film Processing
28%
New Equipment
32%
Film
15%
Rental Equipment
25%

 Use the circle graphs to answer the questions below.

1. How much did the camera club plan to spend on film?

   _____

2. How much more money did the club spend on film?

   _____

3. Why do you think the film-processing supplies cost increased?

   _____

4. What category of their proposed budget was not actually used?

   _____

Extension: After comparing the proposed and actual 1998 budgets for the Camera Club, think about the differences in the figures. Then propose a 1999 budget based on a 10 percent increase for the Camera Club. Draw your proposal on a circle graph. Explain your reasoning for making the budget that you did.

Name _____ Date _____

Point the Way!

A grid is made from a set of evenly spaced horizontal and vertical lines. By naming a pair of numbers, called coordinates, a graph can be made to show a point on a graph. A number pair is written (3,4).

Find whose house is at the coordinate (3,4).

- Start at 0.
- Move 3 spaces right.
- Move 4 spaces up.

The number pair (3,4) shows point B—Barbara's house.

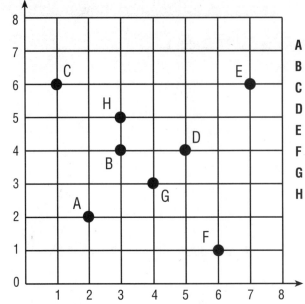

Legend

A	Art's house
B	Barbara's house
C	Claire's house
D	Denny's house
E	Ellen's house
F	Franco's house
G	Gloria's house
H	Hugo's house

 Use the graph to find whose house is at each coordinate.

1. (2,2) _____   2. (1,6) _____   3. (7,6) _____

4. (5,4) _____   5. (6,1) _____   6. (3,5) _____

 Use the graph to find the coordinates of each name.

7. Barbara _____   8. Franco _____   9. Gloria _____

10. Hugo _____   11. Claire _____   12. Denny _____

 Extension: Many city street maps are grids. Find an example of a city grid map and compare it to the number pair graph. How are they alike? How are they different? Can you find the coordinates that tell where you live?

Name _____   Date _____

Which Way Do I Go?

Some grids may have 4 sections. There will be negative numbers naming intersecting lines. Always start at 0. If the first coordinate is negative, move left to that number. If the second coordinate is negative, move down to that number.

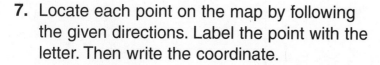

Use the graph to find the coordinate for each location.

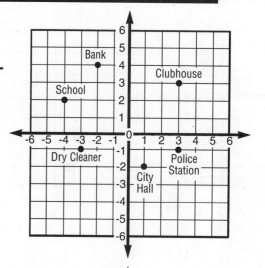

1. bank _____   **2.** police station _____

3. city hall _____   **4.** school _____

5. dry cleaner _____   **6.** clubhouse _____

7. Locate each point on the map by following the given directions. Label the point with the letter. Then write the coordinate.

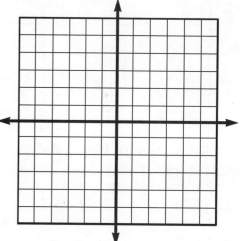

A. Go 3 blocks east and then 4 blocks north.

_____

B. Go 5 blocks east and then 0 blocks north.

_____

C. Go 1 block east and then 1 block south.

_____

D. Go 1 block west and then 2 blocks north.

_____

E. Go 5 blocks west and then 1 block south.

_____

F. Go 4 blocks east and then 4 blocks south.

_____

 Extension: Think about important points of interest or landmarks in your community. Draw a grid graph and mark these points on the graph. Write the coordinates. Give a blank grid to a classmate with the coordinates. Can your classmate find the locations?

Graphs: Reading a Grid Graph

       Statistics and Probability 5-6, SV 7479-0

Name _____   Date _____

The Point of Drawing

Coordinates can be used to draw pictures on a graph. You do not need to write the letters on the graph—only the points.

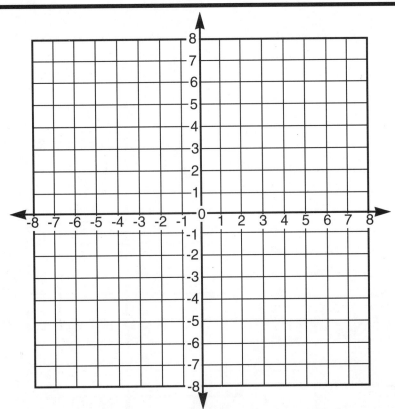

Use the coordinates to make a picture on the graph. Mark each point in the order given. Draw lines between the points with a ruler as you go.

1. (1,5)   **2.** (1,2)   **3.** (2,2)   **4.** (2,-2)   **5.** (3,-2)

6. (3,-6)   **7.** (-3,-6)   **8.** (-3,-2)   **9.** (-2,-2)   **10.** (-2,2)

11. (-1,2)   **12.** (-1,5)   **13.** (1,5)

 Extension: Make your own grid picture. Write the coordinates. Ask a classmate to draw the picture on a separate sheet of paper.

Name _____ Date _____

Riddled with Letters

Check the numbers in each pair carefully. Remember that if the first number is negative, you move left. If the second number is negative, you move down.

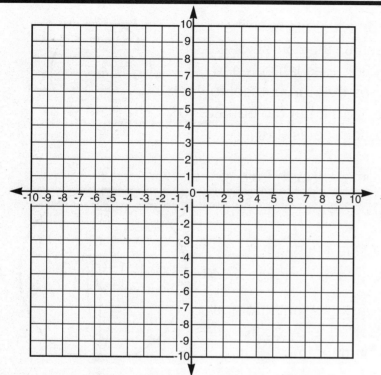

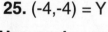 Use the number pairs to mark the points on the grid.

1. (5,5) = A   **2.** (1,10) = B   **3.** (-3,3) = C   **4.** (10,6) = D
5. (5,2) = E   **6.** (-7,-5) = F   **7.** (7,-9) = G   **8.** (-5,-1) = H
9. (8,4) = I   **10.** (2,4) = J   **11.** (9,-4) = K   **12.** (10,1) = L
13. (6,-1) = M   **14.** (8,-7) = N   **15.** (-2,3) = O   **16.** (-2,-6) = P
17. (-9,8) = Q   **18.** (4,0) = R   **19.** (-5,7) = S   **20.** (-4,-7) = T
21. (0,7) = U   **22.** (2,-9) = V   **23.** (-10,-8) = W   **24.** (-1,1) = X
25. (-4,-4) = Y   **26.** (8,10) = Z

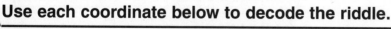 Use each coordinate below to decode the riddle.

Why did the computer go to work out at the gym?

___ ___ ___ ___ ___   ___ ___   ___ ___ ___ ___
(8,4) (-4,-7) (-5,-1) (5,5) (10,6)   (-4,-7) (-2,3)   (-10,-8) (-2,3) (4,0) (9,-4)

___ ___ ___ ___ ___ ___   ___ ___ ___ ___ ___ ___
(-2,3) (-7,-5) (-7,-5) (8,4) (-4,-7) (-5,7)   (-7,-5) (10,1) (-2,3) (-2,-6) (-2,-6) (-4,-4)

 Extension: Use the graph above to send a secret message. Give the code to a classmate to solve.

Graphs: Using a Grid Graph

                                       Statistics and Probability 5-6, SV 7479-0

Name _____   Date _____

Graph the Globe

Longitude and latitude lines are used to help chart a location on Earth. They are imaginary lines that form a grid over the entire Earth.

One of the most important people on an airplane is the navigator. The navigator's job is to chart the course of the airplane. To find location, the navigator uses latitude and longitude lines. Latitudes are the lines that run parallel to each other around the globe horizontally, starting at the equator (0°) and proceeding north and south to both poles (90°).

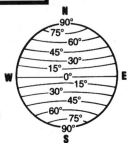

Longitudes are the lines that run from the North Pole to the South Pole, starting at the prime meridian (0°) and encircling the globe (0° to 180°) east to west.

1. Draw and label the longitude lines in the diagram.

Airplane crew members can bring back presents from all over the world. Circle the places referred to by coordinates on the map and write the exercise number in it.

	Latitude	Longitude	Presents
2.	41.2°N	14.9°E	Can of olive oil
3.	39.5°N	116.2°E	Grass skirt
4.	41.5°N	112.2°E	Panda bear
5.	4.6°N	74.1°W	Coffee beans
6.	23.6°S	151.7°E	Koala bear

Extension: What is the latitude and longitude of your community?

Name _____   Date _____

Graphic Pictures

Problem solving with graphs makes information easier to analyze. Pictographs compare data using pictures. Bar graphs are used to compare data. Line graphs are used to show a change in data over time. Circle graphs are used to compare pieces of information to the whole or to other pieces. Grid graphs show locations.

Identify which type of graph would best represent each set of information. Write *pictograph, bar, line, circle,* or *grid.*

1. Kinds of sports preferred by your classmates: _____

2. A family budget: _____

3. Heights of the 5 tallest buildings in the United States: _____

4. Monthly sales of 5 salespeople: _____

5. Population growth of a city during a 10-year period: _____

6. Location of a city's points of interest: _____

7. What type of graph would you use to display this data? Explain your reasoning.

    _____

    _____

Favorite Types of Vehicles

Type	Number of Students
Sedan	7
Van	8
Truck	7
Convertible	15

8. Why would you not use a line graph to display this data? Explain your reasoning.

    _____

    _____

Extension: Your class is giving a play. How could you use each kind of graph during the process of putting it on to help organize data?

Graphs: Choosing Graphs

Statistics and Probability 5-6, SV 7479-0

Name _____   Date _____

The Outcome Is Favorable

Probability is the chance that an activity or event will happen. The outcome is the result of the activity or event. Probability can be shown as a fraction.

Three fruit juice varieties, *A*, *B*, and *C*, are being tested by a person who is blindfolded. What is the probability that the person will rank *C* first?

$$\frac{\text{Favorable outcomes}}{\text{Possible outcomes}} = \frac{1}{3}$$

The probability of picking *C* is $\frac{1}{3}$.

A number cube, which has 6 sides, is tossed. Find the outcome of each event below.

1. The number showing is a 3: _____

2. The number showing is odd: _____

3. The number showing is less than 5: _____

4. The number showing is greater than 1: _____

5. The number showing is prime: _____

6. The number showing is less than 8: _____

Suppose these cards are turned facedown and arranged randomly. You pick one card and then return it.

Find the probability of each event. Write a fraction for each probability.

7. Picking the star: _____

8. Picking the circle: _____

9. Picking the flower or line: _____

10. Picking a rounded shape: _____

 Extension: Work with a classmate. Predict how many times the number 4 will show on a number cube if you roll it 50 times. Now take turns rolling the cube. Record your answers. How close were you to your prediction?

Probability: Exploring Probability

Statistics and Probability 5-6, SV 7479-0

Name _____ Date _____

Going for a Spin!

> **When there is more of something in a group, the probability that you will choose that kind of object increases.**

1. How many sections does the spinner have? How many colors?

   _____

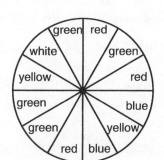

2. What are the possible outcomes of spinning the spinner?

   _____

3. What is the probability of the spinner landing on yellow? on green? on white?

   _____

4. Suppose you are playing a game. You would score a point if the spinner stops on your color. What color would you like to choose?

   _____

5. What are the possible outcomes of the spinner below?

   _____

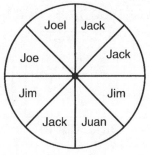

6. What is the probability of the spinner landing on a name with 3 letters in it? 4 letters in it? 5 letters in it?

   _____

Suppose you spin the spinner 8 times. How many times do you think it will land on each name?

7. Joel _____   **8.** Jack _____   **9.** Joe _____   **10.** Jim _____

Extension: Suppose the boys whose names are on the above spinner are playing a game. When the spinner stops on a name, that boy would score a point. Can you predict who would win? Why? Is this game fair? If not, draw a picture of a spinner that would be fair.

Probability: Exploring Probability
Statistics and Probability 5-6, SV 7479-0

Name _____   Date _____

This Is Just Marble-lous!

Mathematical probability is the number you find based on the formula
<u>Favorable outcomes</u>
Possible outcomes

A bag of marbles has 10 white marbles, 5 blue marbles, 40 red marbles, and 25 yellow marbles.

1. What are the possible outcomes? _____

2. What color marble is most likely to be picked?
   Why? _____

Suppose you pick one marble from the bag.
Write the fraction for the mathematical probability that the marble will be each color.

3. blue   **4.** red   **5.** yellow   **6.** white

_____   _____   _____   _____

Now, test the mathematical probability to see if the predicted outcomes are correct. Use colored counters or squares of construction paper to serve as the marbles. Put them in a container. Choose a color 25 times, replacing it each time. Record the data on the table.

Colors Chosen

Color	Tally	Frequency
Blue		
Red		
Yellow		
White		

7. blue   **8.** red   **9.** yellow   **10.** white

_____   _____   _____   _____

11. Did the mathematical probability of outcomes match your test?
    Explain what you found out.

    _____

    _____

Extension: If you continue to test the mathematical probability and choose colors 100 more times, what do you think the outcome would be?

Name _____ Date _____

Card Tricks

When finding the probability of several outcomes happening at once, add the fractions together, then reduce to simplest form if you can.

A	B	C	A	B	C	A	B	C	A
1	2	3	4	5	1	2	3	4	5

Suppose you are playing a game that uses 10 cards. Each card has a number and a letter on it. Because there are 10 cards, there are 10 possible outcomes. What is the probability that you will pick a card with A or 1?

Probability of picking an A = $\frac{4}{10}$ or $\frac{2}{5}$

Probability of picking a 1 = $\frac{2}{10}$ or $\frac{1}{5}$

Probability of picking A or 1 = $\frac{2}{5} + \frac{1}{5} = \frac{3}{5}$

 Answer the questions below.

1. What is the probability that you will pick a card with a B?

   _____

2. What is the probability that you will pick a card with a 5?

   _____

3. What is the probability that you will pick a card with an odd number?

   _____

4. What is the probability that you will pick a card with a B or a 3?

   _____

5. What is the probability that you will pick a card with an A or a B?

   _____

6. What is the probability that you will pick a card with an A, a B, or a 3?

   _____

Extension: Using 10 index cards, make the cards shown above. Now test the mathematical probability. Record your data on a table. What did you find out?

Name _____ Date _____

Frequency Code

Frequency shows the number of times an event happens. Knowing how often something happens can help determine the probability of that event happening.

The most common letter in the English language is the letter *E*. The next most frequently used letters are *T, A, O, I, R,* and *N*. The letters used least often are *Q, Z, K, X,* and *J*.

A	B	C	D	E	F	G	H	I	J	K	L	M

N	O	P	Q	R	S	T	U	V	W	X	Y	Z

1. This is a frequency distribution chart. Fill in the number of times each letter of the alphabet is printed on this page, starting at the beginning of the first paragraph. Do not count the coded paragraph; it is not written in English.

    Knowing the frequency with which letters occur can help you decipher a code. If you see a letter or number often in a coded message, it probably stands for one of the more frequently used letter. Other clues come from short, common words: a single-letter word is usually either *a* or *I*. Two-letter words are commonly *to, in, an, as, at, is,* and so on. If you have found the code for *a*, a two-letter word with *a_* is probably *an, am, as,* or *at*. A very common three-letter word is *the*. By substituting letters whose code you have broken into the coded message, you decode other letters.

2. The message is written in a code in which each letter is substituted for another letter of the alphabet. Fill in the blanks to decode the message. Some blanks have already been filled in to help you. Think about the words you know and about letters that appear next to each other in different places in the words.

Utp imwe zpqp abgwchj igepigbb. G jcqb zghupn um abgw.
Utp imwe ncn hmu zghu um bpu tpq abgw, ixu utpw bpu tpq tcu mhlp.
Etp tcu g tmsp qxh. Hmz pkpqwmhp zghte tpq mh utpcq upgs!

____ boys ____ _____ _____ . __ _____ wanted ___ _____.

____ _____ did ____ _____ __ ____ ___ _____ , but ____ let ____ hit _____.

She ____ __ home ____. ____ everyone _____ ____ ___ ____ _____!

_____

Extension: Create your own code and write a message. Have a classmate break the code.

Name _____ Date _____

Backpack Facts

Probability is sometimes called relative frequency. A table makes it easier to show the ratio of the probable events to the total number of outcomes.

Lucy did a survey of her class. She asked her classmates what color backpack they had. She recorded the results on a table.

Backpack Colors

Color	Number of Students
Blue	8
Red	5
Black	4
Green	7
Gray	6

1. What are the possible outcomes?

   _____

2. What color of backpack is the most popular?

   _____

3. What color of backpack is the least popular?

   _____

4. What is the probability that Karen has a red backpack?

   _____

5. What is the probability that Armando has a gray backpack? _____

6. What is the probability that Larry does not have a blue backpack?

   _____

7. What is the probability that Danielle has a red or green backpack?

   _____

8. What is the probability that Nolan or Anita has a gray backpack?

   _____

 Extension: How does the sample group affect the outcome of the probability? Would the probability be different if Lucy surveyed the whole school? People in a camping equipment store?

Name _____   Date _____

Pets with Proportion

> You can use relative frequencies to make predictions about larger groups.

Hector asked 50 of his classmates how many pets they owned. He made a table to show his data. On the table, he included a column to show frequency outcomes.

Pets Owned

Event	Relative Frequency	Frequency
0 pets	5	$\frac{1}{10}$
1 pet	18	$\frac{9}{25}$
2 pets	20	$\frac{2}{5}$
3 pets	6	$\frac{3}{25}$
4 pets	1	$\frac{1}{50}$
Total	50	1

To predict how many out of 100 students own 3 pets, he wrote a formula, called a proportion, and solved it.

$$\frac{n}{100} = \frac{6}{50}$$

$$n \times 50 = 6 \times 100 \qquad n \times 50 = 600 \qquad n = 12$$

 Answer the questions below.

1. How many out of 100 students own 2 pets? _____

2. How many out of 200 students own 3 pets? _____

3. How many out of 200 students own 2 pets? _____

4. How many out of 100 students own 2 or 3 pets? _____

5. How many out of 200 students own 1 pet? _____

6. How many out of 100 students own fewer than 4 pets? _____

7. How many out of 500 students own 1 pet? _____

8. How many out of 1,000 students own 3 pets? _____

 Extension: How many students are in your school? Using that number for the sample, predict how many pets students own based on Hector's survey.

Name _____ Date _____

Rolling Along

Number shapes, like cubes, are often used when playing games. You can use your probability skills to predict what you will roll.

If you roll a number cube 25 times, how many times do you think each number will show? Make a guess. Then get a number cube and roll it 25 times. Record your information on the table.

Number Cube Probability

Number	Guess	Tally	Relative Frequency	Frequency
1				
2				
3				
4				
5				
6				

 Answer the questions below.

1. Was your guess correct? Why or why not?

   _____

2. Based on your frequency chart, what would you predict your chances are of rolling each number if you toss the dice 100 times?

   1 _____   2 _____   3 _____

   4 _____   5 _____   6 _____

Extension: How would knowing the probabilities of rolling a certain number help you to plan a game strategy? _____

_____

Name _____   Date _____

Your Number's Up!

Mathematical probability is the number found after calculating the outcomes based on the known data. Experimental probability is the number obtained by conducting an experiment.

1. Look at the spinner. Write the probability of an arrow stopping on each number.

   1 _____   2 _____

   3 _____   4 _____

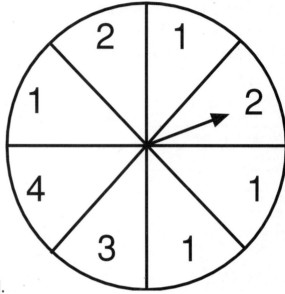

2. Based on the mathematical probability, what is the frequency that an arrow will stop on each number if you spin it 50 times? (HINT: Use proportion.)

   1 _____   2 _____

   3 _____   4 _____

Work with a partner to trace and cut out the spinner shown. Glue it to a piece of cardboard. Use a paper fastener and a paper clip to make a pointer. Spin the pointer 50 times.

3. Record your results on the table below.

Number	Tally	Relative Frequency	Frequency
1			
2			
3			
4			

4. How does the probability of spinning each number compare to the observed probability from your experiment?

_____

 Extension: Is mathematical or experimental probability more appropriate for determining probability?

Name _____   Date _____

A Chance of Rain

To predict probability on a calendar, look at the weather conditions up to that day. Count the total number of days and the number of times each weather occurs.

Look at the weather calendar for May. What are the chances that it will be cloudy on May 11? It was cloudy for 1 day out of the 10 days before the 11th. The chances it will be cloudy on May 11 are $\frac{1}{10}$.

MAY						
Sun.	Mon.	Tues.	Wed.	Thurs.	Fri.	Sat.
1	2	3	4	5	6	7
8	9	10	11	12	13	14
15	16	17	18	19	20	21
22	23	24	25	26	27	28
29	30	31				

Rain

Sunny

Cloudy

 Use the calendar to solve.

1. What is the probability that it will rain on Sunday, May 8?

    _____

2. What is the probability that it will rain on Sunday, May 15?

    _____

3. What is the probability that it will rain on Tuesday, May 24?

    _____

4. What is the probability that it will be cloudy on Saturday, May 14?

    _____

5. What is the probability that it will be cloudy on Sunday, May 22?

    _____

6. What is the probability that it will be sunny on Sunday, May 8?

    _____

 Extension: Record the weather conditions in your area for 2 weeks. Predict the kind of weather you will have on the fifteenth day. Did you predict correctly?

Name _____   Date _____

Oddly Enough!

You can use percentages to express probability.

What do you think the odds are that 2 people in a class of 30 would have the same birthday? To calculate the probability, it is easier to ask the reverse question: What are the odds that every person in the class has a different birthday? The first person can have any birthday at all. The second person must have a birthday on one of the 364 other days in the year. The odds are equal to $\frac{364}{365}$. The third person must have a birthday on one of the 363 days not used up by the first 2 people. This can be written as $\frac{364}{365} \times \frac{363}{365}$.

By the time we complete this procedure for all 30 people, the expression to calculate the chances looks like this: $\frac{364}{365} \times \frac{363}{365} \times \dots \times \frac{336}{365}$.

This expression when calculated is equal to about 0.29. This means that there is a 29% chance that everyone has a different birthday. Therefore, there is a 71% chance that at least 2 people have the same birthday.

Answer the questions below.

1. What is the probability that 2 people in a group of 20 have the same birthday?

   _____

2. What is the largest group possible with less than a 50% chance of 2 people having the same birthday?

   _____

3. What are the chances that 2 people in a group of 20 will have birthdays in the same month?

   _____

4. Despite the calculations, it is difficult to believe that it is so likely that 2 people will have the same birthday. You can prove it again by experimentation. Ask each of your classmates what his or her birthday is. How many do you have to ask before you get 2 dates the same?

   _____

   _____

   _____

Extension: How does a meteorologist use probability to forecast the chances for rain?

Name _____   Date _____

Letter Block

Probability can be expressed as a decimal.

A group of alphabet books is separated into 2 piles. In one pile are the letters *B, D, F, H, L, J, R, O, P, V, G, T, N, Q, C, K.* The other pile contains the letters *I, F, M, P, A, G, W, R, E.*

 Answer the questions below.

1. How many letters do the piles have in common? What are they?

_____

2. What is the probability that a letter chosen from the first pile will be the same as a letter in the second pile? To find the answer to this question, divide the number of letters both piles have by the total amount of blocks in the first pile. Write the answer as a decimal.

_____

3. In Exercise 2 you found the probability of choosing a letter from the first pile that is a letter in the second pile. Now find the probability as a decimal of choosing a letter from the second pile that will be the same as a letter in the first pile.

_____

4. From which pile is there a better chance that a letter chosen will be the same as a letter in the other pile?

_____

The following blocks are added to the first pile: *I, X, Y, Z.*

5. Find the new probability of choosing a letter from the first pile that is the same as a letter in the second pile.

_____

Extension: When naming probability chances, why do most people name them in terms of percentages instead of decimals or fractions?

Name _____ Date _____

Are You Certain?

There are some probabilities in which you know the outcome. This kind of probability is called a certainty!

In most probability examples, you can never be certain what the outcome will be.

Two outcomes are possible if you flip a coin: it will land heads or tails. You write the probability as a number.

$$\frac{1 \text{ head on a penny}}{2 \text{ sides on a penny}} = \frac{1}{2}$$

Suppose you have a trick penny with heads on both sides. You can be certain you will always flip heads. You can also be certain that you will never flip tails. Look at the probabilities for flipping heads and tails.

$$\frac{2 \text{ heads on a trick penny}}{2 \text{ sides on a trick penny}} = \frac{2}{2} \qquad \frac{0 \text{ tails on a trick penny}}{2 \text{ heads on a trick penny}} = \frac{0}{2}$$

If both numbers are the same, or if one of the numbers is 0, the probability is always certain.

Write each probability. Write *certainty* when the outcome is certain.

1. You have a coin that has 2 green sides. You want to flip the coin with the red side up; with the green side up.

   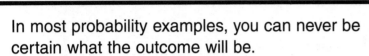

   _____

2. Look at the spinner. You want the spinner to land on 2; on 3. _____

   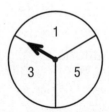

3. Write the letters *R, A, N, D, Y* on 5 pieces of paper and put them in a hat. Pick an *A* from the hat. Pick a *Z* from the hat.

   _____

   R   A   N   D   Y

Extension: Write a case in which the outcome is a certainty. Write a case in which the outcome is open to chance.

Name _____   Date _____

Time for a Combination

Combinations are made by finding all the different ways to group a set of items.

To find how many combinations can be made, multiply the number of first choices by the number of second choices.

1. Mark has 4 sweaters and 3 shirts that can be worn in any combination. How many shirt-sweater combinations can he make?

_____

2. Dustin has 5 kinds of crackers and 3 kinds of cheese. How many cracker-cheese combinations can he make?

_____

3. A sailor can send messages by displaying flags of different colors. He has a flag staff that has room for 3 flags. He has 4 flags that can be used for the top position, 3 flags that can be used for the middle position, and 2 flags that can be used for the bottom position. How many combinations of flag positions can he use?

_____

4. Good Eats Diner is serving a choice of 4 meats, 4 vegetables, and 2 desserts. How many meal combinations can be made?

_____

5. Students at Greenwood Intermediate School are holding student-council elections. Three people are running for president, 3 for vice-president, 2 for treasurer, and 2 for secretary. How many possible combinations of student-council officers are there?

_____

 Extension: Do you have choices of foods in your cafeteria? If so, how many different combinations can you make?

Name _____ Date _____

Combination Lockout!

Combinations can be used to help find the probability of an event happening.

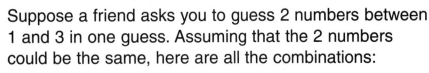

To guess a number between 1 and 20 in one try, your odds are 1 of 20 or $\frac{1}{20}$.

If you are given 4 chances to guess 2 numbers between 1 and 20, your odds are now $\frac{4}{20}$ or $\frac{1}{5}$.

Suppose a friend asks you to guess 2 numbers between 1 and 3 in one guess. Assuming that the 2 numbers could be the same, here are all the combinations:

1 and 1   2 and 1   3 and 1

1 and 2   2 and 2   3 and 2

1 and 3   2 and 3   3 and 3

Since there are 9 combinations of 2 numbers, you have a 1 in 9 chance of guessing the 2 numbers on the first try. There is an easier way to figure this out.

You have 3 choices for the first number and 3 choices for the second number. Multiply 3 x 3 to find the possible combinations. With only 1 guess, your odds are $\frac{1}{9}$.

Suppose that you are asked to guess 3 numbers, each between 1 and 10.

1. What are your odds of guessing all 3 numbers on the first try? Explain your reasoning.

    _____

    _____

    _____

2. You are told that the second number is 7. Now what are your odds of guessing the 3-number combination?

    _____

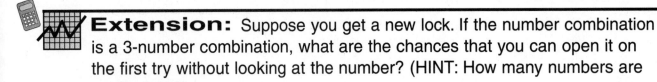

Extension: Suppose you get a new lock. If the number combination is a 3-number combination, what are the chances that you can open it on the first try without looking at the number? (HINT: How many numbers are on the lock?)

Branching Out with Sports

A tree diagram can help you list all the different combinations of a group of items.

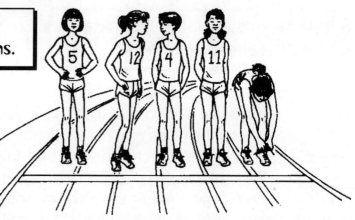

Calvin has tickets for track and field events. He has to choose which events to attend since some are scheduled at the same time.

10:00—mile run, hurdles
11:00—long jump, 100-m run, high jump
12:00—shot-put, pole vault

 Draw a tree diagram that shows the combinations of events he can attend.

 Extension: Choose 2 shirts and 2 pairs of pants that you have. Suppose you could wear them in any combination. Show the combinations of outfits you can wear on a tree diagram.

Name _____ Date _____

The Family Odds

> A table can help you list all the different combinations of a group of items.

Mr. and Mrs. Cleet have dark hair. Of their children, Pete, Claire, and Dot have dark hair, and Clint has red hair. The color of their hair is determined by 2 genes. A gene is the part of a cell that determines the characteristics or traits you inherited from your parents. Possible gene combinations can be shown on a table similar to a multiplication table. In the table at the right, D is the gene for dark hair and r is the gene for red. The gene for dark hair is dominant, which means that any pair of genes with at least one D will produce dark hair. The gene for red hair is recessive, meaning that both genes must be the same for the characteristic to appear. The pairs of letters within the table are the possible combinations, or genotypes, the children could inherit.

		Mr. Cleet	
		D	r
Mrs. Cleet	D	DD	Dr
	r	Dr	rr

1. What genotype did Clint Cleet inherit? _____

2. What 2 possible genotypes did Claire inherit? _____

You can find the probability of parents with genotype Dr having a child with dark hair. Divide the number of genotypes that produce dark hair by the total number of possible combinations. This is $\frac{3}{4}$ and means there are 3 children of 4 who are likely to have dark hair.

If one parent has dark hair and one parent has red hair, there are 2 possible gene tables. Complete the tables.

3.
	D	r
r		
r		

4.
	D	D
r		
r		

5. In Exercise 3, what is the probability of the parents having a red-haired child?
_____ of _____

6. In Exercise 4, what is the probability of the parents having a red-haired child?
_____ of _____

 Extension: Another inherited trait is an attached or unattached earlobe. Research to find out which is dominant. Then use tables to determine probability of having that feature. Take an experimental test of your classmates to compare mathematical and experimental probability. What did you find out?

Name _____   Date _____

Fruitful Combinations

A combination is a set of items. A total combination is
the total number of ways you can show these items.
You do not have to use all the items in each combination.

Look at the foods. You can group them 7 different ways.

1   **2**   **3**   **4**   **5**   **6**   **7**

Solve.

1. Linda has an apple and an orange. She
   wants to figure out all the possible ways to
   eat the fruit. List the total combinations.

   _____

2. Marcus is painting a fruit picture for art
   class. He has 4 fruits: a plum, a pear, a kiwi,
   and a banana. List the total combinations
   Marcus can paint.

   _____

   _____

   _____

3. How could knowing combinations help you
   to predict an outcome?

   _____

   _____

Extension: What are your favorite fruits? Name at least 3. Write the
total combinations you could make to eat them.

Name _____   Date _____

Find Your Order!

Permutations are ways of putting things together in a set
where order is important. There are many more possible
combinations when order is important.

In a school parking lot, there are only 2 spaces
available for 3 cars: a red car, a blue car, and a
silver car. How many combinations are there?

   red, blue   blue, silver   red, silver

There are 3 possible combinations for parking the cars.
Because order is not important, red and blue is the same
as blue and red. It only counts as one combination.

If order is important, you can use permutations to
put combinations together. The permutations for
parking the 3 cars in the 2 spaces are listed below:

   red, blue   blue, silver   red, silver

   blue, red   silver, blue   silver, red

 Solve. Do not use any unit more than once in each permutation.

1. Write the permutations for the letters
   in the word *sun*.

   _____

2. Dan uses 3 signal flags to send
   messages. The flags are white,
   green, and yellow. He uses 2 flags
   for each message. Write all of the
   permutations for signal flags.

   _____

3. Ally is trying to figure out the code
   for a number lock. The code is a 2-
   digit number. She can use only the
   numbers 0, 1, 2, and 3. Write all the
   permutations.

   _____

 Extension: Car license plates use permutations of letters and
numbers in order to make many combinations. Can you think of other items in
which letters and numbers are used in permutations?

Name _____ Date _____

It's a Toss-up

> Drawing a picture of all the possible permutations makes it easier to find the probability that an outcome will happen.

Tien-ho has 2 coins. What is the chance of both coins coming up tails? He draws a picture to help find all the permutations. *T* is tails and *H* is heads.

Two tails is 1 of the 4 ways the coins can land. The likelihood of both coins coming up tails is 1 out of 4, $\frac{1}{4}$.

1. What is the likelihood of both coins coming up heads? _____

2. What is the likelihood of 1 coin coming up heads and 1 coin coming up tails? _____

Now suppose you toss 3 coins. There are 8 different ways the coins can land. Write *T* or *H* on each coin to show the different ways.

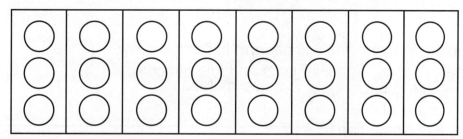

3. What is the likelihood of 3 coins coming up tails? _____

4. What is the likelihood of 2 coins coming up tails and 1 coin coming up heads? _____

Extension: Suppose you have 2 number cubes. Draw a picture to show the number combinations you could roll. Write some questions about the probabilities. Ask a classmate to solve them using your drawing.

Probability: Making Permutations
© Steck-Vaughn Company   89   Statistics and Probability 5-6, SV 7479-0

Name _____ Date _____

Setting the Facts Straight

If you only need to know how many ways you can
arrange a group of items, you can use factorials
to find how many combinations you can make.

Salina is setting a table. She uses a factorial to find the ways to arrange
the 3 utensils. She multiples 1 x 2 x 3. The product of 1 x 2 x 3 = 6.
She can arrange the utensils on the table 6 different ways.

 Write the factorial and solve.

1. The art class is having an art show. Holly has 4 paintings to show.
   Each painting has a differently shaped frame. She wants to arrange
   her paintings in the most interesting way. How many ways can she
   arrange them?

   _____

2. Mr. Noce is arranging dancers who will perform in the art show.
   There will be Greek, African, Spanish, jazz, and folk dancers.
   How many ways can Mr. Noce arrange them?

   _____

3. Renie and Jose each made 4 clay pots for the art show.
   They are all different shapes and sizes. How many ways can
   they arrange them?

   _____

 Extension: How many ways can your class line up?

Name _____   Date _____

Depending on the Outcome

There are 2 kinds of probability—independent probability and dependent probability.

Suppose you flip a penny. You have 1 chance of flipping heads and 1 chance of flipping tails. You can write the probability of flipping heads or tails like this: $\frac{1}{2}$. No matter how many times you flip the penny, the probability of flipping heads or tails is always $\frac{1}{2}$. This type of probability is independent.

Suppose you have 2 blue marbles and 1 pink marble in a bag. The chance of picking a pink marble is $\frac{1}{3}$. If you pick a blue marble, only a blue marble and pink marble will be left. The probability of picking a pink marble is now $\frac{1}{2}$. The probability has changed. It depends on how many marbles are left in the bag. This type of probability is dependent.

 Solve.

The guests at Judy's party play a game. Each person rolls a number cube. The numbers on the cube are 1 to 6. The person who rolls the highest number goes first.

1. What is the probability that Judy will roll a 6? Is this probability dependent or independent?

   _____

2. What is the probability that Anna will roll a 6? Is this probability dependent or independent?

   _____

Each person at the party chooses a balloon out of a bag. The balloon holds 5 blue balloons and 1 red balloon.

3. Jorge picks the first balloon. What is the probability it is blue? Is the probability of picking the first balloon dependent or independent?

   _____

4. After Jorge picks, there are 4 blue balloons and 1 red balloon left. What is the probability that Jerri will pick a blue balloon?

   _____

 Extension: List other examples of dependent and independent probability.

Name _____   Date _____

Game-Time Wins

When answering word problems dealing with probability, be sure you understand what the question asks.

 Answer the problems below.

1. Ben, Nancy, Hakim, and Shanda are playing a board game called Come Get Your Money. To see who goes first, they write their names on paper and put them into a box. What is the probability that Shanda will get to go first?

   _____

2. Ben rolls a number cube. He wants to roll a 6 so he can draw a Bank Card to get some money. What is his chance of rolling a 6 in one roll?

   _____

3. Nancy must roll 1 or 2 or she will lose all of her money. What are Nancy's chances of rolling 1 or 2 in one roll?

   _____

4. Hakim is about to land on Bankruptcy Square. He must roll 1, 2, or 6 on the number cube to avoid this space. What is his chance of rolling one of those numbers in one roll?

   _____

5. Shanda lands on a free spot. She can use 1, 2, or 3 Bank Cards to earn extra money. How many total combinations can she make with the cards she has?

   _____

6. Ben lost all of his money, so he is out of the game. What is the probability that Hakim will win?

   _____

Extension: Play a board game with several classmates. Take turns posing probability questions to predict the chances of different events happening.

Statistics and Probability Grades 5-6
Answer Key

p. 13 1.

Temperatures in Chicago

Temperature	Tally	Frequency
16	II	2
17	III	3
18	II	2
19	I	1
21	IIII	5
22	II	2
24	I	1
25	II	2
26	II	2

2. 20 3. winter 4. 10 degrees 5. 20.65 or 21 6. 21
7. 21 8. 3 9. Answers will vary. 10. Answers will vary.
11. No; answers will vary. 12. yes; The group is
limited and Ray sampled a large portion of that group.

p. 14 1.

2.

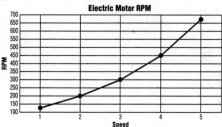

3.

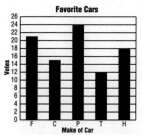

p. 15 1. Donald, Carol, Joan, Steve, Christy 2. yes
3. 1/5 4. 2/5 5. 0 6. 3/8 7. 1/4 8. 1/8 9. 1/2 10. 5/8
11. 3/8 12. 1/2 13. 1/2 14. 1/4 15. 0

p. 16 1. July 2. dolphins 3. 28 4. June 5. finback,
baleen, humpback, dolphins

p. 17 1. Phantoms 2. Chargers 3. 20 4. Cheetahs and
Bulldogs 5. Answers may vary. Chargers;
The Chargers have had the most wins for the season.

p. 18 1. Tables may vary slightly.

World Waterfalls

Waterfall	Country	Height
Wollomombi Falls	Australia	1,580 feet
Takakkaw Falls	Canada	1,600 feet
Sutherland Falls	New Zealand	1,904 feet
Kukenaam Falls	Venezuela	2,050 feet
Tigela Falls	South Africa	2,800 feet
Angel Falls	Venezuela	3,212 feet

2. Angel Falls 3. Wollomombi Falls 4. Kukenaam
Falls, Tigela Falls, Angel Falls 5. Answers will vary.
Possible answer: Venezuela is very mountainous and
has many rivers.

p. 19 1. Tables may vary slightly.

Beginners		Intermediates		Advanced Swimmers		Champion Swimmers	
Starfish	12	Guppies	7	Swordfish	18	Canoeing Class	10
Polliwogs	12	Minnows	8	Tunas	15	Water Sports	14
Tadpoles	12	Sunfish	9	Flying Fish	20	Life Saving	13

2. 36 3. Advanced Swimmers 4. 150

p. 20 Tables may vary slightly.

1.

Sandwiches Sold

	Monday	Wednesday	Friday
Bologna	23	19	27
Ham	57	46	67
Turkey	36	20	51

2. 15 3. 69 4. 145 5. Answers will vary.

p. 21 1. 10:00 A.M. 2. 3 hours 45 minutes 3. Phoenix,
Billings, Los Angeles 4. Los Angeles 5. 12:15 P.M.

p. 22 Answers will vary. These are reasonable
answers.

Dish	How Much	Estimated Cooking Time	Starting Time	Estimated Serving Time
Soup	4 cups	10 min	4:50 PM	5:00 PM
Beef	5.37 pounds	2 hrs, 45 min	2:25 PM	5:10 PM
Potatoes	4	55 min	4:15 PM	5:10 PM
Beans	4 cups	15 min	4:55 PM	5:10 PM
Dessert	6 baked apples	65 min	4:40 PM	5:45 PM

p. 23

	Jacqueline	Patricia	Louis	Emanuel
Chess	0	X	X	X
Reading	X	X	0	X
Swimming	X	X	X	0
Kite Flying	X	0	X	X

1. chess 2. kite flying 3. reading 4. swimming

p. 24

	Hamburger	Spaghetti	Egg Rolls	Tacos
Sherry	0	X	X	X
Jerry	X	X	0	X
Merry	X	0	X	X
Perry	X	X	X	0

1. hamburgers 2. egg rolls 3. spaghetti 4. tacos

p. 25

Punch Recipe for a Crowd

Ingredient	25 People	50 People	100 People	200 People
Orange juice	2 quarts	4 quarts	8 quarts	16 quarts
Pineapple juice	1 1/2 cups	3 cups	6 cups	12 cups
Apple juice	1 quart	2 quarts	4 quarts	8 quarts

1. 4 gallons 2. 1 gallon 3. 6 3/4 gallons 4. 1/2 container.

p. 26

Seeds Sold

Packets Sold	Cost	Team Earns
1	$0.50	$0.15
2	$1.00	$0.30
3	$1.50	$0.45
4	$2.00	$0.60
5	$2.50	$0.75
6	$3.00	$0.90
7	$3.50	$1.05
and so on		

1. $0.45 2. 5 packets 3. $1.05 4. 23 packets
5. 20 packets

p. 27 1. Kareem 2. 5 3. game 2 4. 54

5.

	Kareem	Delia	Ling	Stacy
Game 1	7	2	5	1
Game 2	5	5	5	5
Game 3	10	5	1	3

p. 28 Answers and tables will vary. Accept all reasonable answers.

p. 29 1.

How Students Get to School

Transportation	Tally	Frequency
Bus	IIII	4
Bike	THL I	6
Car	THL	5
Walk	III	3

2.

Where Students Live

Location	Tally	Frequency
Bank St.	THL	5
Mill St.	THL II	7
Front St.	THL I	6

3.-4. Answers will vary.

p. 30 1. No; He should check cartons in the middle and at the bottom. 2. No; The 10 he found represent the 200 shipped. 3. No: His sample was based on an abnormal situation. 4. Yes; The 1 he found represented 50 eggs out of the whole group.

p. 31 1. No; Not enough people were sampled.
2. Answers will vary. No; because the people were employees of the company. Yes; A large group of people were asked. 3. No; The people sampled might be loyal to the company they work for. 4. Answers will vary. Possible answer: Survey shoppers in the soup aisle of a grocery store.

p. 32 1. 35 2. 60 3. 15 4. 200

p. 33 1.-5. Answers will vary.

p. 34 Answers will vary.

p. 35 1. 23 travel books 2. children's books
3. children's books 4. week 1

p. 36 1. .240 2. 21 3. 9 4. 45 5. .360

p. 37 1. 14, 14, 14, 13, 13, 12, 12, 12, 12, 10, 9, 9
2. 12 3. 1, 1, 2, 2, 3, 3, 4, 4, 5, 5, 5, 5 4. 5 5. Answers will vary.

p. 38 1. 11, 28, 60, 70; 44 2. 50 3. 13 4. 50
5. Answers will vary.

p. 39 1. $294 2. $414 3. $31 4. $239 5.-6. Answers will vary.

p. 40 1. 10 2. Ben and Anil 3. Crissy 4. 80 5. 350
6. The number of actual votes was rounded to the nearest ten.

p. 41 1. full-2 hours; 3/4-1 1/2 hour; 1/2-1 hour; 1/4-1/2 hour 2. 9 hours; 2 1/2 hours 3. 12 1/2 more hours
4. 15 1/2 hours 5. 6 more hours 6. Answers will vary.

p. 42

Cars Manufactured

State	Number	Rounded Number
Michigan	2,031,000	2,000,000
Delaware	531,000	500,000
Missouri	524,000	500,000
Georgia	481,000	500,000
Illinois	403,000	400,000
New Jersey	374,000	400,000
Oklahoma	329,000	300,000
Wisconsin	322,000	300,000

Cars Manufactured

State	Cars
Michigan	20 cars
Delaware	5 cars
Missouri	5 cars
Georgia	5 cars
Illinois	4 cars
New Jersey	4 cars
Oklahoma	3 cars
Wisconsin	3 cars

p. 43 1. Book Nook; 200 2. Book Nook; 50
3. adventure 4. adventure 5. 1,600 6. Answers will vary.

p. 44 1. 1986 2. 1985 3. 1987 4., The bar for 1985 is longer, so it is easier to read.

p. 45 1. 5,000 2. Austin 3. Miami 4. Yes; he sold 22,000 shirts in all four stores. 5. $66,000 6. Answers will vary.

p. 46 1.

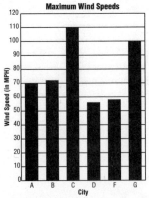

2. Hatteras 3. 54 mph 4. No; The graph title indicates that the data is only the maximum wind speed for one time, not an average over a period of time.

p. 47 1. thousands 2. January 3. About 70,000
4.

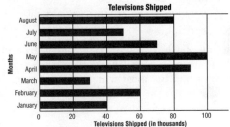

Statistics and Probability 5-6, SV 7479-0

p. 48 1. a. 2. c. 3. Scale shows intervals of 100.

p. 49 1.

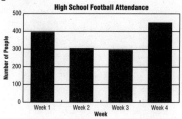

2. week 4 3. Weeks 2 and 3 4. 361 people

p. 50 1.

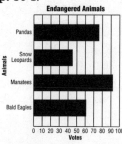

2. pandas 3. 153 4. 274 5. Most reasonable response: Manatees; More students favored manatees in the survey.

p. 51 1. 1.-4., answers will vary.

p. 52 1. 550 2. Pine Ridge 3. 50 4. 1,400 5. both schools 6. Pine Ridge-$70; Marble Creek-$67.50

p. 53 1. noon 2. 10 A.M. and 11:00 A.M. 3. 10° 4. 20°; The graph trend shows that the temperature rises 2° most hours.

p. 54 1.

2. Thursday to Friday in Week 1 3. The number was the same. 4. Monday and Tuesday 5. Fridays and Saturdays; Possible answer: Most people do not have to work the next day.

p. 55 1. Possible answer: 20 tickets 2. Raffle Ticket Sales 3. vertical-Tickets Sold; Horizontal-Month 4. Graphs may vary.

p. 56 1.

Photolink Inc. 1998 Quarterly Sales

Quarter	Photos Sold
1	900
2	960
3	870
4	1,200

2.

3. The number of photo sales continued to increase.
4. 983 photos per quarter

p. 57 1.

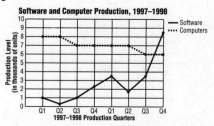

2. The trend is for increase, except for 2nd-quarter drops in 1998. 3. The trend is for general decrease in production levels. 4. no

p. 58 1.-2. Check students' graphs.

p. 59 1. After-School Activities 2. It's labeled with 3 activities and the number of students involved in each. 3. 40 4. 1/4 5. Half as many students prefer television viewing as sports. 6. Rita would show 3 equal sections, each taking up 1/3 of the circle.

p. 60 1. 126 2. 104 3. 14 4. 20% 5. 40% 6. 40%

p. 61 1. summer school 2. working 3.-4., Answers will vary.

p. 62 1. $60 2. 1/12 3. 5/12 4. 1/6 5. 1/3

6.

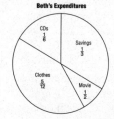

p. 63 1. $1,014 2. $253.50 3. It increased because the club used more film. 4. Advertising

p. 64 1. Art's 2. Claire's 3. Ellen's 4. Denny's 5. Franco's 6. Hugo's 7. (3,4) 8. (6,1) 9. (4,3) 10. (3,5) 11. (1,6) 12. (5,4)

p. 65 For 1. (-2,4) 2. (3, -1) 3. (1,-2) 4. (-4,2) 5. (-3,-1)
6. (3,3) 7. A. (3,4) B. (5,0) C. (1,-1) D. (-1, 2) E. (-5,-1)
F. (4, -4)

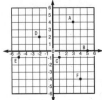

p. 66 1.-13.

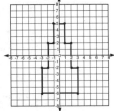

p. 67 1.-26.,

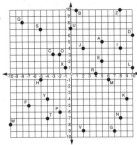

Riddle: IT HAD TO WORK OFF ITS FLOPPY.

p. 68 1.

Answers 2.-6.: Check students' maps.

p. 69 1. pictograph 2. circle graph 3. bar graph
4. bar graph 5. line graph 6. grid graph 7. Bar graph
or pictograph; The data can be compared easily.
8. Line graphs show change over time.

p. 70 1. 1/6 2. 1/2 3. 2/3 4. 5/6 5. 2/3 6. 1 7. 1/8
8. 1/8 9. 1/4 10. 3/8

p. 71 1. 12; 5 2. red, blue, green, yellow, white 3. 2/12
or 1/6; 4/12 or 1/3; 1/12 4. green; There are more
chances of the spinner stopping on green since it has
more sections. 5. Jack, Jim, Juan, Joe, Joel 6. 3/8;
5/8; 0 7. 1 time 8. 3 times 9. 1 time 10. 2 times

p. 72 1. white, blue, red, yellow 2. red; because there
are more red marbles than any other color. 3. 5/80 or
1/16 4. 40/80 or 1/2 5. 25/80 or 5/16 6. 10/80 or 1/8
7.-11., Answers will vary.

p. 73 1. 3/10 2. 2/10 or 1/5 3. 6/10 or 3/5 4. 5/10 or
1/2 5. 7/10 6. 9/10

p. 74 1.

A	B	C	D	E	F	G	H	I	J	K	L	M
70	24	29	42	151	24	17	59	71	2	7	48	25

N	O	P	Q	R	S	T	U	V	W	X	Y	Z
70	86	15	6	70	72	122	33	6	21	3	22	2

2. The boys were playing baseball. A girl wanted to
play. The boys did not want to let her play, but they let
her hit once. She hit a home run. Now everyone wants
her on their team.

p. 75 1. blue, red, black, green, gray 2. blue 3. black
4. 5/30 or 1/6 5. 6/30 or 1/5 6. 22/30 or 11/15 7. 12/30
or 2/5 8. 6/30 or 1/5

p. 76 1. 40 2. 24 3. 80 4. 52 5. 72 6. 98 7. 180
8. 120

p. 77 1.-2., Answers will vary.

p. 78 1. 1/2; 1/4; 1/8; 1/8 2. 25; 12.5 or 13; 6.25 or 6;
6.25 or 6 3.-4., Answers will vary.

p. 79 1. 1/7 2. 2/14 3. 6/23 4. 3/13 5. 6/21 6. 1/7

p. 80 1. 40% 2. 22 3. 100% 4. Answers will vary.

p. 81 1. 4; F, P, G, R 2. 0.25 3. 0.44 4. second pile
5. 0.25

p. 82 1. 0/2-certainty; 2/2-certainty 2. 0/3-certainty;
1/3 3. 1/5; 0/5-certainty

p. 83 1. 12 2. 15 3. 24 4. 32 5. 36

p. 84 1. 1/1,000. Since you have 10 choices for all 3
numbers, your possible combinations are 10 x 10 x 10,
or 1,000. You have 1 try, so your odds are 1/1000.
2. 10 x 1 x 10, or 100 possible combinations; 1/100

p. 85 1.

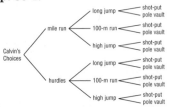

p. 86 1. rr 2. DD, Dr

	D	r
r	Dr	rr

	D	D
r	Dr	Dr

3.
	D	r
r	Dr	rr

4.
	D	D
r	Dr	Dr

5. 2 of 4 or 1 of 2 6. 0

p. 87 1. apple; orange; apple and orange 2. plum;
pear; kiwi; banana; plum and pear; plum and kiwi;
plum and banana; pear and kiwi; pear and banana;
kiwi and banana; plum, pear, and kiwi; plum, pear,
and banana; plum, kiwi, and banana; pear, kiwi, and
banana; plum, pear, kiwi, and banana 3. By knowing
all the combinations, you can easily predict
mathematical probability.

p. 88 1. sun; snu; uns; usn; nus; nsu 2. white, green;
white, yellow; yellow, green; green, yellow; yellow,
white; green, white 3. 01; 10; 02; 20; 03; 30; 12; 21; 13;
31; 23; 32

p. 89 1. 1/4 2. 1/2
Row 1: T, T, T, H, T, H, H, H
Row 2: T, T, H, T, H, T, H, H
Row 3: T, H, T, T, H, H, T, H
3. 1/8 4. 3/8

p. 90 1. 1 x 2 x 3 x 4 = 24 2. 1 x 2 x 3 x 4 x 5 = 120
3. 1 x 2 x 3 x 4 x 5 x 6 x 7 x 8 = 40,320

p. 91 1. 1/6; independent 2. 1/6; independent 3. 5/6;
independent 4. 4/5

p. 92 1. 1/4 2. 1/6 3. 1/3. 4. 1/2 5. 7 8. 1/3

Statistics and Probability 5-6, SV 7479-0